C-1932

ISBN 0-8373-1932-3

THE PASSBOOK® SERIES

MAR 2 8 2001

PASSBOOKS®

FOR

CAREER OPPORTUNITIES

PRINCIPAL LIBRARY CLERK

National Learning Corporation

212 Michael Drive, Syosset, New York 11791

(516) 921-8888

Copyright © 1998 by

National Learning Corporation

212 Michael Drive, Syosset, New York 11791
(516) 921-8888

PRINTED IN THE UNITED STATES OF AMERICA

PASSBOOK SERIES®

THE *PASSBOOK SERIES*® has been created to prepare applicants and candidates for the ultimate academic battlefield—the examination room.

At some time in our lives, each and every one of us may be required to take an examination—for validation, matriculation, admission, qualification, registration, certification, or licensure.

Based on the assumption that every applicant or candidate has met the basic formal educational standards, has taken the required number of courses, and read the necessary texts, the *PASSBOOK SERIES*® furnishes the one special preparation which may assure passing with confidence, instead of failing with insecurity. Examination questions—together with answers—are furnished as the basic vehicle for study so that the mysteries of the examination and its compounding difficulties may be eliminated or diminished by a sure method.

This book is meant to help you pass your examination provided that you qualify and are serious in your objective.

The entire field is reviewed through the huge store of content information which is succinctly presented through a provocative and challenging approach—the question-and-answer method.

A climate of success is established by furnishing the correct answers at the end of each test.

You soon learn to recognize types of questions, forms of questions, and patterns of questioning. You may even begin to anticipate expected outcomes.

You perceive that many questions are repeated or adapted so that you gain acute insights, which may enable you to score many sure points.

You learn how to confront new questions, or types of questions, and to attack them confidently and work out the correct answers.

You note objectives and emphases, and recognize pitfalls and dangers, so that you may make positive educational adjustments.

Moreover, you are kept fully informed in relation to new concepts, methods, practices, and directions in the field.

You discover that you are actually taking the examination all the time: you are preparing for the examination by "taking" an examination, not by reading extraneous and/or supererogatory textbooks.

In short, this PASSBOOK®, used directedly, should be an important factor in helping you to pass your test.

BASIC FUNDAMENTALS OF FILING SCIENCE

CONTENTS

———

FILING

EXAMINATION SECTION

CONTENTS

———

CODING

EXAMINATION SECTION

CONTENTS

PHILOSOPHY, PRINCIPLES, PRACTICES, AND TECHNICS
OF
SUPERVISION, ADMINISTRATION, MANAGEMENT, AND ORGANIZATION
CONTENTS

CONTENTS (cont'd)

BASIC FUNDAMENTALS OF LIBRARY SCIENCE

CONTENTS

PRINCIPAL LIBRARY CLERK

DUTIES

Supervises clerical employees and independently performs important specialized clerical work in the circulation, reference, cataloging or administrative departments of a public library. Assists a Librarian in charging and discharging books, registering, borrowers, collecting fines, reserving books and answering the more difficult questions concerning the library's collections and services while working at the circulation and reference desks. Supervises the preparation of overdue notices, catalog cards and filing of shelf list cards; oversees and revises the pasting and lettering of new books; prepares books and magazines for the bindery. Supervises the maintenance of records and assists in the preparation of bills, purchase orders, payroll and statistical reports for the main and branch libraries. Performs related work as required.

SCOPE OF THE EXAMINATION

The written test will be designed to test for knowledge, skills, and/or abilities in such areas as:

1. Library terminology and practices;
2. Office practices;
3. Understanding and interpreting written material;
4. Supervision;
5. English usage; and
6. Record keeping and data interpretation.

HOW TO TAKE A TEST

I. YOU MUST PASS AN EXAMINATION

A. *WHAT EVERY CANDIDATE SHOULD KNOW*

Examination applicants often ask us for help in preparing for the written test. What can I study in advance? What kinds of questions will be asked? How will the test be given? How will the papers be graded?

As an applicant for a civil service examination, you may be wondering about some of these things. Our purpose here is to suggest effective methods of advance study and to describe civil service examinations.

Your chances for success on this examination can be increased if you know how to prepare. Those "pre-examination jitters" can be reduced if you know what to expect. You can even experience an adventure in good citizenship if you know why civil service examinations are given.

B. *WHY ARE CIVIL SERVICE EXAMINATIONS GIVEN?*

Civil service examinations are important to you in two ways. As a citizen, you want public jobs filled by employees who know how to do their work. As a job-seeker, you want a fair chance to compete for that job on an equal footing with other candidates. The best known means of accomplishing this two-fold goal is the competitive examination.

Examinations are widely publicized throughout the nation. They may be administered for jobs in federal, state, city, municipal, town, or village governments or agencies.

Any citizen may apply, with some limitations, such as the age or residence of applicants. Your experience and education may be reviewed to see whether you meet the requirements for the particular examination. When these requirements exist, they are reasonable and are applied consistently to all applicants. Thus, a competitive examination may cause you some uneasiness now, but it is your privilege and safeguard.

C. *HOW ARE CIVIL SERVICE EXAMINATIONS DEVELOPED?*

Examinations are carefully written by trained technicians who are specialists in the field known as "psychological measurement," in consultation with recognized authorities in the field of work that the test will cover. These experts recommend the subject matter areas or skills to be tested; only those knowledges or skills important to your success on the job are included. The most reliable books and source materials available are used as references. Together, the experts and technicians judge the difficulty level of the questions.

Test technicians know how to phrase questions so that the problem is clearly stated. Their ethics do not permit "trick" or "catch" questions. Questions may have been tried out on sample groups, or subjected to statistical analysis, to determine their usefulness.

Written tests are often used in combination with performance tests, ratings of training and experience, and oral interviews. All of these measures combine to form the best known means of finding the right man for the right job.

II. HOW TO PASS THE WRITTEN TEST

A. *NATURE OF THE EXAMINATION*

To prepare intelligently for civil service examinations, you should know how they differ from school examinations you have taken. In school you were assigned certain definite pages to read or subjects to cover. The examination questions were quite detailed and usually emphasized memory. Civil service examinations, on the other hand, try to discover your present ability to perform the duties of a position, plus your potentiality to learn these duties. In other words, a civil service examination attempts to predict how successful you will be. Questions cover such a broad area that they cannot be as minute and detailed as school examination questions.

In the public service similar kinds of work, or positions, are grouped together in one "class." This process is known as "position-classification." All the positions in a class are paid according to the salary range for that class. One class title covers all these positions, and they are all tested by the same examination.

B. *FOUR BASIC STEPS*

1. Study the Announcement.--How, then, can you know what subjects to study? Our best answer is: "Learn as much as possible about the class of positions for which you have applied." The examination will test the knowledge, skills, and abilities needed to do the work.

Your most valuable source of information about the position you want is the official announcement of the examination. This announcement lists the training and experience qualifications. Check these standards and apply only if you come reasonably close to meeting them.

The brief description of the position in the examination announcement offers some clues to the subjects which will be tested. Think about the job itself. Review the duties in your mind. Can you perform them, or are there some in which you are rusty? Fill in the blank spots in your preparation.

Many jurisdictions preview the written test in the examination announcement by including a section called "Knowledge and Abilities Required," "Scope of Examination," or some similar heading. Here you will find out specifically what fields will be tested.

2. Review Your Own Background.-- Once you learn in general what the position is all about, and what you need to know to do the work, ask yourself which subjects you already know fairly well and which need improvement. You may wonder whether to concentrate on improving your strong areas or on building some background in your fields of weakness. When the announcement has specified "some knowledge" or "considerable knowledge," or has used adjectives such as "beginning principles of ...." or "advanced .....methods," you can get a clue as to the number and difficulty of questions to be asked in any given field. More questions, and hence broader coverage, would be included for those subjects which are more important in the work. Now weigh your strengths and weaknesses against the job requirements and prepare accordingly.

3. Determine the Level of the Position.-- Another way to tell how intensively you should prepare is to understand the level of the job for which you are applying. Is it the entering level? In other words, is this the position in which beginners in a field of work are hired? Or is it an intermediate or advanced level? Sometimes this is indicated by such words as "Junior" or "Senior" in the class title.Other jurisdictions use Roman numerals to designate the level: Clerk I,

Clerk II, for example. The word "Supervisor" sometimes appears in the title. If the level is not indicated by the title, check the description of duties. Will you be working under very close supervision, or will you have responsibility for independent decisions in this work?

    4. Choose Appropriate Study Materials.-- Now that you know the subjects to be examined and the relative amount of each subject to be covered, you can choose suitable study materials. For beginning level jobs, or even advanced ones, if you have a pronounced weakness in some aspect of your training, read a modern, standard textbook in that field. Be sure it is up-to-date and has general coverage. Such books are normally available at your library, and the librarian will be glad to help you locate one. For entry level positions, questions of appropriate difficulty are chosen -- neither highly advanced questions, nor those too simple. Such questions require careful thought but not advanced training.

    If the position for which you are applying is technical or advanced, you will read more advanced, specialized material. If you are already familiar with the basic principles of your field, elementary textbooks would waste your time. Concentrate on advanced textbooks and technical periodicals. Think through the concepts and review difficult problems in your field.

    These are all general sources. You can get more ideas on your own initiative, following these leads. For example, training manuals and publications of the government agency which employs workers in your field can be useful, particularly for technical and professional positions. A letter or visit to the government department involved may result in more specific study suggestions, and certainly will provide you with a more definite idea of the exact nature of the position you are seeking.

III. KINDS OF TESTS

    Tests are used for purposes other than measuring knowledge and ability to perform specified duties. For some positions, it is equally important to test ability to make adjustments to new situations or to profit from training. In others, basic mental abilities not dependent upon information are essential. Questions which test these things may not appear as pertinent to the duties of the position as those which test for knowledge and information. Yet they are often highly important parts of a fair examination. For very general questions, it is almost impossible to help you direct your study efforts. What we can do is to point out some of the more common of these general abilities needed in public service positions and describe some typical questions.

    1. General Information

    Broad, general information has been found useful for predicting job success in some kinds of work. This is tested in a variety of ways, from vocabulary lists to questions about current events. Basic background in some field of work, such as sociology or economics, may be sampled in a group of questions. Often these are principles which have become familiar to most persons through "exposure" rather than through formal training. It is difficult to advise you how to study for these questions; being alert to the world around you is our best suggestion.

2. Verbal Ability

An example of an ability needed in many positions is verbal or language ability. Verbal ability is, in brief, the ability to use and understand words. Vocabulary and grammar tests are typical measures of this ability. "Reading comprehension" or "paragraph interpretation" questions are common in many kinds of civil service tests. You are given a paragraph of written material and asked to find its central meaning.

3. Numerical Ability

Number skills can be tested by the familiar arithmetic problem, by checking paired lists of numbers to see which are alike and which are different, or by interpreting charts and graphs. In the latter test, a graph may be printed in the test booklet which you are asked to use as the basis for answering questions.

4. Observation

A popular test for law-enforcement positions is the observation test. A picture is shown to you for several minutes, then taken away. Questions about the picture test your ability to observe both details and larger elements.

5. Following Directions

In many positions in the public service, the employee must be able to carry out written instructions dependably and accurately. You may be given a chart with several columns, each column listing a variety of information. The questions require you to carry out directions involving the information given in the chart.

6. Skills and Aptitudes

Performance tests effectively measure some manual skills and aptitudes. When the skill is one in which you are trained, such as typing or shorthand, you can practice. These tests are often very much like those given in business school or high school courses. For many of the other skills and aptitudes, however, no short-time preparation can be made. Skills and abilities natural to you or that you have developed throughout your lifetime are being tested.

Many of the general questions just described provide all the data needed to answer the questions and ask you to use your reasoning ability to find the answers. Your best preparation for these tests, as well as for tests of facts and ideas, is to be at your physical and mental best. You, no doubt, have your own methods of getting into an exam-taking mood and keeping "in shape." The next section lists some ideas on this subject.

IV. KINDS OF QUESTIONS

Only rarely is the "essay" question, which you answer in narrative form, used in civil service tests. Civil service tests are usually of the short-answer type. Full instructions for answering these questions will be given to you at the examination. But in case this is your first experience with short-answer questions and separate answer sheets, here is what you need to know.

1. Multiple-Choice Questions

Most popular of the short-answer questions is the "multiple-choice" or "best-answer" question. It can be used, for example, to test for factual knowledge, ability to solve problems, or judgment in meeting situations found at work.

A multiple-choice question is normally one of three types:

(1) It can begin with an incomplete statement followed by several possible endings. You are to find the one ending which *best* completes the statement, although some of the others may not be entirely wrong.

(2) It can also be a complete statement in the form of a question which is answered by choosing one of the statements listed.

(3) It can be in the form of a problem -- again you select the best answer.

Here is an example of a multiple-choice question with a discussion which should give you some clues as to the method for choosing the right answer.

SAMPLE QUESTION:

When an employee has a complaint about his assignment, the action which will *best* help him overcome his difficulty is
   (A) to discuss his difficulty with his co-workers
   (B) to take the problem to the head of the organization
   (C) to take the problem to the person who gave him the assignment
   (D) to say nothing to anyone about his complaint

In answering this question you should study each of the choices to find which is best. Consider choice (A). Certainly an employee may discuss his complaint with fellow employees, but no change or improvement can result, and the complaint remains unsolved. Choice (B) is a poor choice since the head of the organization probably does not know what assignment you have been given, and taking your problem to him is known as "going over the head" of the supervisor. The supervisor, or person who made the assignment, is the person who can clarify it or correct any injustice. Choice (C) is, therefore, correct. To say nothing, as in choice (D), is unwise. Supervisors have an interest in knowing the problems employees are facing, and the employee is seeking a solution to his problem.

2. True-False Questions

The "true-false" or "right-wrong" form of question is sometimes used. Here a complete statement is given. Your problem is to decide whether the statement is right or wrong.

SAMPLE QUESTION:

A person-to-person long distance telephone call costs less than a station-to-station call to the same city.

This question is wrong, or "false," since person-to-person calls are more expensive.

This is not a complete list of all possible question forms, although most of the others are variations of these common types. You will always get complete directions for answering questions. Be sure you understand *how* to mark your answers -- ask questions until you do.

V. RECORDING YOUR ANSWERS

For an examination with very few applicants, you may be told to record your answers in the test booklet itself. Separate answer sheets are much more common. If this separate answer sheet is to be scored by machine -- and this is often the case -- it is highly important that you mark your answers correctly in order to get credit.

An electric test-scoring machine is often used in civil service offices because of the speed with which papers can be scored. Machine-scored answer sheets must be marked with a special pencil, which will be given to you. This pencil has a high graphite content which responds to the electrical scoring machine. As a matter of fact, stray dots may register as answers, so do not let your pencil rest on the answer sheet while you are pondering the correct answer. Also, if your pencil lead breaks or is otherwise defective, ask for another.

Since the answer sheet will be dropped in a slot in the scoring machine, be careful not to bend the corners or get the paper crumpled.

The answer sheet normally has five vertical columns of numbers, with 30 numbers to a column. These numbers correspond to the question numbers in your test booklet. After each number, going across the page, are four or five pairs of dotted lines. These short dotted lines have small letters or numbers above them. The first two pairs may also have a "T" and "F" above the letters. This indicates that the first two pairs only are to be used if the questions are of the true-false type. If the questions are multiple-choice, disregard this "T" and "F" completely, and pay attention only to the small number or letters.

Answer your questions in the manner of the sample that follows. Proceed in the sequential steps outlined below.

Assume that you are answering question 32, which is:

    32. The largest city in the United States is:
        A. Washington, D.C.   B. New York City   C. Chicago
        D. Detroit   E. San Francisco

1. Choose the answer you think is best.
    New York City is the largest, so choice B is correct.
2. Find the row of dotted lines numbered the same as the question you are answering.
    This is question number 32, so find row number 32.
3. Find the pair of dotted lines corresponding to the answer you have chosen.
    You have chosen answer B, so find the pair of dotted lines marked "B".
4. Make a solid black mark between the dotted lines.
    Go up and down two or three times with your pencil so plenty of graphite rubs off, but do not let the mark get outside or above the dots.

VI. BEFORE THE TEST

Common sense will help you find procedures to follow to get ready for an examination. Too many of us, however, overlook these sensible measures. Indeed, nervousness and fatigue have been found to be the most serious reasons why applicants fail to do their best on civil service tests. Here is a list of reminders.

1. Begin Your Preparation Early

     Don't wait until the last minute to go scurrying around for books and materials or to find out what the position is all about.

2. Prepare Continuously

     An hour a night for a week is better than an all-night cram session. This has been definitely established. What is more, a night a week for a month will return better dividends than crowding your study into a shorter period of time.

3. Locate the Place of the Examination

     You have been sent a notice telling you when and where to report for the examination. If the location is in a different town or otherwise unfamiliar to you, it would be well to inquire the best route and learn something about the building.

4. Relax the Night Before the Test

     Allow your mind to rest. Do not study at all that night. Plan some mild recreation or diversion; then go to bed early and get a good night's sleep.

5. Get Up Early Enough to Make a Leisurely Trip to the Place for the Test

     Then unforeseen events, traffic snarls, unfamiliar buildings, will not upset you.

6. Dress Comfortably

     A written test is not a fashion show. You will be known by number and not by name, so wear something comfortable.

7. Leave Excess Paraphernalia at Home

     Shopping bags and odd bundles will get in your way. You need bring only the items mentioned in the official notice sent to you; usually everything you need is provided. Do not bring reference books to the examination. They will only confuse those last minutes and be taken away from you when in the test room.

8. Arrive Somewhat Ahead of Time

     If because of transportation schedules you must get there very early, bring a newspaper or magazine to take your mind off yourself while waiting.

9. Locate the Examination Room

     When you have found the proper room, you will be directed to the seat or part of the room where you will sit. Sometimes you are given a sheet of instructions to read while you are waiting. Do not fill out any forms until you are told to do so; just read them and be ready.

10. Relax and Prepare to Listen to the Instructions

11. If you have any physical problem that may keep you from doing your best, be sure to tell the test administrator. If you are sick, or in poor health, you really cannot do your best on the test. You can come back and take the test some other time.

VII. AT THE TEST

   The day of the test is here and you have the test booklet in your hand. The temptation to get going is very strong. Caution! There is more to success than knowing the right answers. You must know how to identify your papers and understand variations in the type of short-answer question used in this particular examination. Follow these suggestions for maximum results from your efforts:

1. Cooperate with the Monitor

The test administrator has a duty to create a situation in which you can be as much at ease as possible. He will give instructions, tell you when to begin, check to see that you are marking your answer sheet correctly. He is not there to guard you, although he will see that your competitors do not take unfair advantage. He wants to help you do your best.

2. Listen to All Instructions

Don't jump the gun! Wait until you understand all directions. In most civil service tests you get more time than you need to answer the questions. So don't get in a hurry. Read each word of instructions until you clearly understand the meaning. Study the examples. Listen to all announcements. Follow directions. Ask questions if you do not understand what to do.

3. Identify Your Papers

Civil service examinations are usually identified by number only. You will be assigned a number; you must not put your name on your test papers. Be sure to copy your number correctly. Since more than one examination may be given, copy your exact examination title.

4. Plan Your Time

Unless you are told that a test is a "speed" or "rate-of-work" test, speed itself is not usually important. Time enough to answer all the questions will be provided. But this does not mean that you have all day. An overall time limit has been set. Divide the total time (in minutes) by the number of questions to get the approximate time you have for each question.

5. Do Not Linger Over Difficult Questions

If you come across a difficult question, mark it with a paper clip (useful to have along) and come back to it when you have been through the booklet. One caution if you do this -- be sure to skip a number on your answer sheet too. Check often to be sure that you have not lost your place and that you are marking in the row numbered the same as the question you are answering.

6. Read the Questions

Be sure you know what the question asks! Many capable people are unsuccessful because they failed to *read* the questions correctly.

7. Answer All Questions

Unless you have been instructed that a penalty will be deducted for incorrect answers, it is better to guess than to omit a question.

8. Speed Tests

It is often better *not* to guess on speed tests. It has been found that on timed tests people are tempted to spend the last few seconds before time is called in marking answers at random -- without even reading them -- in the hope of picking up a few extra points. To discourage this practice, the instructions may warn you that your score will be "corrected" for guessing. That is, a penalty will be applied. The incorrect answers will be deducted from the correct ones, or some other penalty formula will be used.

9. Review Your Answers

If you finish before time is called, go back to the questions you guessed or omitted to give further thought to them. Review other answers if you have time.

10. Return Your Test Materials

If you are ready to leave before others have finished or time is called, take *all* your materials to the monitor and leave quietly. Never take any test material with you. The monitor can discover whose papers are not complete, and taking a test booklet may be grounds for disqualification.

VIII. EXAMINATION TECHNIQUES

1. Read the *general* instructions carefully. These are usually printed on the first page of the examination booklet. As a rule, these instructions refer to the timing of the examination; the fact that you should not start work until the signal and must stop work at a signal, etc. If there are any *special* instructions, such as a choice of questions to be answered, make sure that you note this instruction carefully.

2. When you are ready to start work on the examination, that is as soon as the signal has been given, read the instructions to each question booklet, underline any key words or phrases, such as *least, best, outline, describe,* and the like. In this way you will tend to answer as requested rather than discover on reviewing your paper that you *listed without describing,* that you selected the *worst* choice rather than the *best* choice, etc.

3. If the examination is of the objective or so-called multiple-choice type, that is, each question will also give a series of possible answers: A, B, C, or D, and you are called upon to select the best answer and write the letter next to that answer on your answer paper, it is advisable to start answering each question in turn. There may be anywhere from 50 to 100 such questions in the three or four hours allotted and you can see how much time would be taken if you read through all the questions before beginning to answer any. Furthermore, if you come across a question or a group of questions which you know would be difficult to answer, it would undoubtedly affect your handling of all the other questions.

4. If the examination is of the esssay-type and contains but a few questions, it is a moot point as to whether you should read all the questions before starting to answer any one. Of course if you are given a choice, say five out of seven and the like, then it is essential to read all the questions so you can eliminate the two which are most difficult. If, however, you are asked to answer all the questions, there may be danger in trying to answer the easiest one first because you may find that you will spend too much time on it. The best technique is to answer the first question, then proceed to the second, etc.

5. Time your answers. Before the examination begins, write down the time it started, then add the time allowed for the examination and write down the time it must be completed, then divide the time available somewhat as follows:

   (a) If $3\frac{1}{2}$ hours are allowed, that would be 210 minutes. If you have 80 objective-type questions, that would be an average of $2\frac{1}{2}$ minutes per question. Allow yourself no more than 2 minutes per question, or a total of 160 minutes, which will permit about 50 minutes to review.

   (b) If for the time allotment of 210 minutes, there are 7 essay questions to answer, that would average about 30 minutes a question. Give yourself only 25 minutes per question so that you have about 35 minutes to review.

6. The most important instruction is *to read each question* and make sure you know what is wanted. The second most important instruction is to *time yourself properly* so that you answer every question. The third most important instruction is to *answer every question*. Guess if you have to but include something for each question. Remember that you will receive no credit for a blank and will probably receive some credit if you write something in answer to an essay question. If you guess a letter, say "B" for a multiple-choice question, you may have guessed right. If you leave a blank as the answer to a multiple-choice question, the examiners may respect your feelings but it will not add a point to your score.

7. Suggestions
   a. <u>Objective-Type Questions</u>
      (1) Examine the question booklet for proper sequence of pages and questions.
      (2) Read all instructions carefully.
      (3) Skip any question which seems too difficult; return to it after all other questions have been answered.
      (4) Apportion your time properly; do not spend too much time on any single question or group of questions.
      (5) Note and underline key words -- *all, most, fewest, least, best, worst, same, opposite*.
      (6) Pay particular attention to negatives.
      (7) Note unusual option, e.g., unduly long, short, complex, different or similar in content to the body of the question.
      (8) Observe the use of "hedging" words -- *probably, may, most likely, etc.*
      (9) Make sure that your answer is put next to the same number as the question.
     (10) Do not second-guess unless you have good reason to believe the second answer is definitely more correct.
     (11) Cross out original answer if you decide another answer is more accurate; do not erase.
     (12) Answer all questions; guess unless instructed otherwise.
     (13) Leave time for review.
   b. <u>Essay-Type Questions</u>
      (1) Read each question carefully.
      (2) Determine exactly what is wanted. Underline key words or phrases.
      (3) Decide on outline or paragraph answer.
      (4) Include many different points and elements unless asked to develop any one or two points or elements.
      (5) Show impartiality by giving pros and cons unless directed to select one side only.
      (6) Make and write down any assumptions you find necessary to answer the question.
      (7) Watch your English, grammar, punctuation, choice of words.
      (8) Time your answers; don't crowd material.

8. Answering the Essay Question
   Most essay questions can be answered by framing the specific response around several key words or ideas. Here are a few such key words or ideas:

M's: manpower, materials, methods, money, management;

P's: purpose, program, policy, plan, procedure, practice, problems, pitfalls, personnel, public relations.

a. <u>Six Basic Steps in Handling Problems</u>:

(1) **Preliminary** plan and background development

(2) Collect information, data and facts

(3) Analyze and interpret information, data and facts

(4) Analyze and develop solutions as well as make recommendations

(5) Prepare report and sell recommendations

(6) Install recommendations and follow up effectiveness

b. <u>Pitfalls to Avoid</u>

(1) *Taking things for granted*

A statement of the situation does not necessarily imply that each of the elements is necessarily true; for example, a complaint may be invalid and biased so that all that can be taken for granted is that a complaint has been registered.

(2) *Considering only one side of a situation*

Wherever possible, indicate several alternatives and then point out the reasons you selected the best one.

(3) *Failing to indicate follow-up*

Whenever your answer indicates action on your part, make certain that you will take proper follow-up action to see how successful your recommendations, procedures, or actions turn out to be.

(4) *Taking too long in answering any single question*

Remember to time your answers properly.

IX. AFTER THE TEST

Scoring procedures differ in detail among civil service jurisdictions although the general principles are the same. Whether the papers are hand-scored or graded by the electric scoring machine we have described, they are nearly always graded by number. That is, the person who marks the paper knows only the number -- never the name -- of the applicant. Not until all the papers have been graded will they be matched with names. If other tests, such as training and experience or oral interview ratings have been given, scores will be combined. Different parts of the examination usually have different weights. For example, the written test might count 60 percent of the final grade, and a rating of training and experience 40 percent. In many jurisdictions, veterans will have a certain number of points added to their grades.

After the final grade has been determined, the names are placed in grade order and an eligible list is established. There are various methods for resolving ties between those who get the same final grade: probably the most common is to place first the name of the person whose application was received first. Job offers are made from the eligible list in the order the names appear on it.

You will be notified of your grade and your rank order as soon as all these computations have been made. This will be done as rapidly as possible.

People who are found to meet the requirements in the announcement are called "eligibles." Their names are put on a list of eligibles. An eligible's chances of getting a job depend on how high he stands on this list and how fast agencies are filling jobs from the list.

When a job is to be filled from a list of eligibles, the agency asks for the names of people on the list of eligibles for that job.

When the civil service commission receives this request, it sends to the agency the names of the three people highest on the list. Or, if the job to be filled has specialized requirements, the office sends the agency, from the general list, the names of the top three persons who meet those requirements.

The appointing officer makes a choice from among the three people whose names were sent to him. If the selected person accepts the appointment, the names of the others are put back on the list to be considered for future openings.

That is the rule in hiring from all kinds of eligible lists, whether they are for typist, carpenter, chemist, or something else. For every vacancy, the appointing officer has his choice of any one of the top three eligibles on the list. This explains why the person whose name is on top of the list sometimes does not get an appointment when some of the persons lower on the list do. If the appointing officer chooses the No.2 or No.3 eligible, the No.1 eligible does not get a job at once, but stays on the list until he is appointed or the list is terminated.

X. HOW TO PASS THE INTERVIEW TEST

The examination for which you applied requires an oral interview test. You have already taken the written test and you are now being called for the interview test -- the final part of the formal examination.

You may think that it is not possible to prepare for an interview test and that there are no procedures to follow during an interview.

Our purpose is to point out some things you can do in advance that will help you and some good rules to follow and pitfalls to avoid while you are being interviewed.

A. WHAT IS AN INTERVIEW SUPPOSED TO TEST?

The written examination is designed to test the technical knowledge and competence of the candidate; the oral is designed to evaluate intangible qualities, not readily measured otherwise, and to establish a list showing the relative fitness of each candidate, *as measured against his competitors,* for the position sought. Scoring is not on the basis of "right" or "wrong," but on a sliding scale of values ranging from "not passable" to "outstanding." As a matter of fact, it is possible to achieve a relatively low score without a single "incorrect" answer because of evident weakness in the qualities being measured,

Occasionally, an examination may consist entirely of an oral test -- either an individual or a group oral. In such cases, information is sought concerning the technical knowledges and abilities of the candidate, since there has been no written examination for this purpose. More commonly, however, an oral test is used to supplement a written examination.

B. WHO CONDUCTS INTERVIEWS?

The composition of oral boards varies among different jurisdictions. In nearly all, a representative of the personnel department serves as chairman. One of the members of the board may be a representative of the department in which the candidate would work. In some cases, "outside experts" are used, and, frequently, a business man or some other representative of the general public is asked to serve. Labor and management or other special groups may be represented. The aim is to secure the services of experts in the appropriate field.

However the board is composed, it is a good idea (and not at all improper or unethical) to ascertain in advance of the interview who the members are and what groups they represent. When you are introduced to them, you will have some idea of their backgrounds and interests, and at least you will not stutter and stammer over their names.

C. *WHAT TO DO BEFORE THE INTERVIEW*

While knowledge about the board members is useful and takes some of the surprise element out of the interview, there is other preparation which is more substantive. It *is* possible to prepare for an oral -- in several ways:

1. Keep a Copy of Your Application and Review it Carefully Before the Interview

   This may be the only document before the oral board, and the starting point of the interview. Know what experience and education you have listed there, and the sequence and dates of it. Sometimes the board will ask *you* to review the highlights of your experience for them; you should not have to hem and haw doing it.

2. Study the Class Specification and the Examination Announcement

   Usually, the oral board has one or both of these to guide them. The qualities,characteristics,or knowledges required by the position sought are stated in these documents. They offer valuable clues as to the nature of the oral interview. For example, if the job involves supervisory responsibilities, the announcement will usually indicate that knowledge of modern supervisory methods and the qualifications of the candidate as a supervisor will be tested. If so, you can expect such questions, frequently in the form of a hypothetical situation which you are expected to solve. *Never* go into an oral without knowledge of the duties and responsibilities of the job you seek.

3. Think Through Each Qualification Required

   Try to visualize the kind of questions *you* would ask if you were a board member. How well could you answer them? Try especially to appraise your own knowledge and background in each area, *measured against the job sought*, and identify any areas in which you are weak. Be critical and realistic -- do not flatter yourself.

4. Do Some General Reading in Areas in Which You Feel You May be Weak

   For example, if the job involves supervision and your past experience has *not*, some general reading in supervisory methods and practices, particularly in the field of human relations, might be useful. *Do not*, study agency procedures or detailed manuals. The oral board will be testing your understanding and capacity, *not* your memory.

5. Get a Good Night's Sleep and Watch Your General Health and Mental Attitude

   You will want a clear head at the interview. Take care of a cold or other minor ailment, and, of course, *no hangovers*.

D. WHAT TO DO THE DAY OF THE INTERVIEW

Now comes the day of the interview itself. Give yourself plenty of time to get there. Plan to arrive somewhat ahead of the scheduled time, particularly if your appointment is in the fore part of the day. If a previous candidate fails to appear, the board might be ready for you a bit early. By early afternoon an oral board is almost invariably behind schedule if there are many candidates, and you may have to wait. Take along a book or magazine to read, or your application to review. But leave any extraneous material in the waiting room when you go in for your interview. In any event, relax and compose yourself.

The matter of dress is important. The board is forming impressions about you -- from your experience, your manners, your attitudes, and from your appearance. Give your personal appearance careful attention. Dress your *best*, but not your flashiest. Choose conservative, appropriate clothing, and be sure it and you are immaculate. This is a business interview, and your appearance should indicate that you regard it as such. Besides, being well-groomed and properly dressed will help boost your confidence.

Sooner or later, someone will call your name and escort you into the interview room. *This is it.* From here on you are on your own. It is too late for any more preparation. But, remember, you asked for this opportunity to prove your fitness, and you are here because your request was granted.

E. WHAT HAPPENS WHEN YOU GO IN?

The usual sequence of events will be as follows: The clerk (who is often the board stenographer) will introduce you to the chairman of the oral board, who will introduce you to each other member of the board. Acknowledge the introductions before you sit down. Do not be surprised if you find a microphone facing you or a stenotypist sitting by. Oral interviews are usually recorded, in the event of an appeal or other review.

Usually the chairman of the board will open the interview by reviewing the highlights of your education and work experience from your application -- primarily for the benefit of the other members of the board, as well as to get the material into the record. Do not interrupt or comment unless there is an error or significant misinterpretation; if so, do not hesitate. But do not quibble about insignificant matters. Usually, also, he will ask you some question about your education, your experience, or your present job -- partly to get you started talking, to establish the interviewing "rapport." He may start the actual questioning, or turn it over to one of the other members. Frequently each member undertakes the questioning on a particular area, one in which he is perhaps most competent. So you can expect each member to participate in the examination. And because the time is limited, you may expect some rather abrupt switches in the direction the questioning takes. Do not be upset by it. Normally, a board member will not pursue a single line of questioning unless he discovers a particular strength or weakness.

After each member has participated, the chairman will usually ask whether any member has any further questions, then will ask you if you have anything you wish to add. Unless you are expecting this question, it may floor you. Or worse, it may start you off on an extended, extemporaneous speech. The board is not usually seeking more information. The question is principally to offer you a last opportunity to present further qualifications or to indicate that you have nothing to add. So, if you feel that a significant qualification or characteristic has been overlooked, it is proper to point it out in a sentence or so. Do not compliment the board on the thoroughness of their examination -- they have been sketchy, and you know it. If you wish, merely say, "No thank you, I have nothing further to add." This is a point where you can "talk yourself out" of a good impression or fail to present an important bit of information. *Remember, you close the interview yourself*.

The chairman will then say,"That is all,Mr.Smith,thank you." Do not be startled; the interview is over, and quicker than you think. Say,"Thank you and good morning," gather up your belongings and take your leave. Save your sigh of relief for the other side of the door.

F. *HOW TO PUT YOUR BEST FOOT FORWARD*

Throughout all this process, you may feel that the board individually and collectively is trying to pierce your defenses, to seek out your hidden weaknesses, and to embarrass and confuse you. Actually, this is not true. They are obliged to make an appraisal of your qualifications for the job you are seeking, and they *want to see you in your best light*. Remember, they must interview all candidates and a noncooperative candidate may become a failure in spite of their best efforts to bring out his qualifications. Here are fifteen(15) suggestions that will help you:

1. Be Natural. Keep Your Attitude Confident,But Not Cocky

If *you* are not confident that you can do the job, do not ex-expect the *board* to be. Do not apologize for your weaknesses, try to bring out your strong points. The board is interested in a positive, not a negative presentation. Cockiness will antagonize any board member, and make him wonder if you are covering up a weakness by a false show of strength.

2. Get Comfortable, But Don't Lounge or Sprawl

Sit erectly but not stiffly. A careless posture may lead the board to conclude you are careless in other things, or at least that you are not impressed by the importance of the occasion to you.Either conclusion is natural, even if incorrect. Do not fuss with your clothing, or with a pencil or an ashtray. Your hands may occasionally be useful to emphasize a point; do not let them become a point of distraction.

3. Do Not Wisecrack or Make Small Talk

This is a serious situation, and your attitude should show that you consider it as such. Further, the time of the board is limited; they do not want to waste it, and neither should you.

4. Do Not Exaggerate Your Experience or Abilities

In the first place, from information in the application,from other interviews and other sources, the board may know more about you than you think; in the second place, you probably will not get away with it in the first place. An experienced board is rather adept at spotting such a situation. Do not take the chance.

5. If You Know a Member of the Board, Do Not Make a Point of It, Yet Do Not Hide It.

Certainly you are not fooling him, and probably not the other members of the board. Do not try to take advantage of your acquaintanceship -- it will probably do you little good.

6. Do Not Dominate the Interview

Let the board do that. They will give you the clues -- do not assume that you have to do all the talking. Realize that the board has a number of questions to ask you, and do not try to take up all the interview time by showing off your extensive knowledge of the answer to the first one.

15

7. Be Attentive

You only have twenty minutes or so, and you should keep your attention at its sharpest throughout. When a member is addressing a problem or a question to you, give him your undivided attention. Address your reply principally to him, but do not exclude the other members of the board.

8. Do Not Interrupt

A board member may be stating a problem for you to analyze. He will ask you a question when the time comes. Let him state the problem, and wait for the question.

9. Make Sure You Understand the Question

Do not try to answer until you are sure what the question is. If it is not clear, restate it in your own words or ask the board member to clarify it for you. But do not haggle about minor elements.

10. Reply Promptly But Not Hastily

A common entry on oral board rating sheets is "candidate responded readily," or "candidate hesitated in replies." Respond as promptly and quickly as you can, but do not jump to a hasty, ill-considered answer.

11. Do Not Be Peremptory in Your Answers

A brief answer is proper -- but do not fire your answer back. That is a losing game from your point of view. The board member can probably ask questions much faster than you can answer them.

12. Do Not Try To Create the Answer You Think the Board Member Wants

He is interested in what kind of mind you have and how it works -- not in playing games. Furthermore, he can usually spot this practice and will usually grade you down on it.

13. Do Not Switch Sides in Your Reply Merely to Agree With a Board Member

Frequently, a member will take a contrary position merely to draw you out and to see if you are willing and able to defend your point of view. Do not start a debate, yet do not surrender a good position. If a position is worth taking, it is worth defending.

14. Do Not Be Afraid to Admit an Error in Judgment if You Are Shown to Be Wrong

The board knows that you are forced to reply without any opportunity for careful consideration. Your answer may be demonstrably wrong. If so, admit it and get on with the interview.

15. Do Not Dwell at Length on Your Present Job

The opening question may relate to your present assignment. Answer the question but do not go into an extended discussion. You are being examined for a *new* job, not your present one. As a matter of fact, try to phrase *all* your answers in terms of the job for which you are being examined.

G. BASIS OF RATING

Probably you will forget most of these "do's" and "don'ts" when you walk into the oral interview room. Even remembering them all will not insure you a passing grade. Perhaps you did not have the qualifications in the first place. But remembering them *will* help you to put your best foot forward, without treading on the toes of the board members.

Rumor and popular opinion to the contrary notwithstanding, an oral board wants you to make the best appearance possible. They know you are under pressure -- but they also want to see how you respond to it as a guide to what your reaction would be under the pressures of the job you seek. They will be influenced by the degree of poise you display, the personal traits you show, and the manner in which you respond.

EXAMINATION SECTION

EXAMINATION SECTION

DIRECTIONS: Each question or incomplete statement is followed by several suggested answers or completions. Select the one that BEST answers the question or completes the statement. *PRINT THE LETTER OF THE CORRECT ANSWER IN THE SPACE AT THE RIGHT.*

1. Reference materials refer to those materials that   1. ___
   A. circulate
   B. are available for inter-library loan
   C. remain in the library
   D. are strictly for the use of the library staff
   E. are used for professional development

2. The process of identifying a work is USUALLY referred to as 2. ___
   A. descriptive cataloging   B. accessioning
   C. labeling   D. serializing
   E. marketing

3. The *two most widely used* standard lists of subject headings 3. ___
   are:
   A. Sears List of Subject Headings and ALA Rules
   B. Library of Congress Subject Headings and Sears List
      of Subject Headings
   C. Dewey and Sears List of Subject Headings
   D. Library of Congress Subject Headings and Dewey
   E. Sears List of Subject Headings and Haykin's Practical
      Guide to Subject Headings

4. An example of a book catalog is   4. ___
   A. C.B.I.   B. Sears List of Subject Headings
   C. Library of Congress Catalog D. National Union Catalog
   E. Anglo-American Cataloging Rules

5. The Dewey Decimal Classification was developed in 1873 by 5. ___
   A. the Library of Congress   B. John Dewey
   C. Melvil Dewey   D. Samuel Dewey
   E. Thomas E. Dewey

6. The Dewey Decimal Classification is composed of _____ main 6. ___
   classes.
   A. 100   B. 2   C. 50   D. 1000   E. 10

7. The Dewey Decimal Classification number *never* has more than 7. ___
   _____ to the left.
   A. 1 digit   B. 2 digits   C. 3 digits
   D. 4 digits   E. 5 digits

8. To distinguish among books assigned the same classification   8. ___
   number, another number is assigned. This is called a _____
   number.
      A. L.C.   B. N.U.C.   C . title   D. cutter E. call

9. The classification number and the author number *together*   9. ___
   make up the _____ number.
      A. title   B. cutter   C. L.C.   D. call   E. Dewey

10. The *second most frequently used* classification system in the   10. ___
    United States is
       A. Dewey Decimal Classification B. National Union Catalog
       C. Nelinet Classification D. Library of Congress Classification
       E. Sears Classification

11. Reference tools that list books and other materials are   11. ___
    called
       A. encyclopedias   B. compendiums   C. bibliographies
       D. directories   E. almanacs

12. Books that list names of persons or organizations along with   12. ___
    pertinent information about them are called
       A. almanacs   B. encyclopedias of organizations
       C. gazetteers   D. statistical abstracts   E. directories

13. A collection of maps is referred to as a(n)   13. ___
       A. series   B. survey   C. guidebook   D. atlas
       E. gazetteer

14. Descriptive information about cities and countries is usually 14. ___
    found in
       A. atlases   B. guidebooks   C. almanacs
       D. periodicals E. card catalogs

15. Eric Partridge and Harold Wentworth are *best* known for   15. ___
       A. desk encyclopedias   B. unabridged dictionaries
       C. historical dictionaries D. dictionaries of slang
       E. synonyms and antonyms

16. Evans and Fowler are *best* known for   16. ___
       A. dictionaries of current usage B. historical dictionaries
       C. bibliographies   D. abridged dictionaries
       E. synonyms and antonyms

17. Murray and Craigie are *best* known for   17. ___
       A. synonyms and antonyms   B. almanacs
       C. bibliographies   D. dictionaries of current usage
       E. historical dictionaries

18. Funk and Wagnalls, Random House, and Webster's are *best*   18. ___
    known for
       A. historical dictionaries   B. unabridged dictionaries
       C. almanacs   D. abbreviations   E. bibliographies

19. A comprehensive adult encyclopedia with somewhat less   19. ___
    coverage and detail than the Americana or Britannica is
      A. Whitaker's   B. World Almanac   C. Columbia
      D. World Book   E. Collier's

20. A one-volume general encyclopedia with concise information   20. ___
    on a wide range of subjects is
      A. Encyclopedia Americana   B. World Book Encyclopedia
      C. Columbia Encyclopedia   D. Whitaker's Encyclopedia
      E. Collier's Encyclopedia

21. A popular juvenile encyclopedia is   21. ___
      A. Encyclopedia Britannica   B. Americana
      C. Columbia   D. Collier's   E. World Book

22. Bartlett and Stevenson are *best* known for   22. ___
      A. almanacs   B. directories
      C. handbooks of coins and stamps
      D. handbooks of quotations
      E. handbooks of occupations

23. A standard handbook on parliamentary procedure was   23. ___
    authored by
      A. Smith   B. Robert   C. Carter   D. Jones   E. Wright

24. The sheets of a book, sometimes unsewn, issued in advance   24. ___
    of publication for review or promotion purposes, are usual-
    ly referred to as _____ sheets.
      A. courtesy   B. advance   C. preview   D. forward   E. lead

25. In the United States the medal for the *best* picture book   25. ___
    of the year is called the _____ medal.
      A. Illustrator's   B. Caldecott   C. Newbery
      D. Bowker   E. ALA

26. An award presented annually to the author of the MOST dis-   26. ___
    tinguished contribution to American literature for children
    is called the _____ medal.
      A. Caldecott   B. Illustrator's   C. Newbery
      D. Bowker   E. ALA

27. A microfilm reader which can also be used to make enlarge-   27. ___
    ments automatically is called a
      A. xerox machine   B. reader-writer   C. duplicator
      D. reader-printer   E. printer-reader

28. A character, originally in the form of picture-writing en-   28. ___
    graved in stone by the ancient Egyptians to convey thoughts
    or information, is called
      A. hierophant   B. hierograph   C. hieroglyph
      D. hieratic   E. hierodule

29. The science of control and communication processes in ani-   29. ___
    mals and machines is referred to as
      A. interjection   B. interpolation   C. instrumentation
      D. cybernetics   E. symbiosis

30. The bookbinding process which gives the book a convex 30. ___
    spine is called
        A. spining   B. rounding   C. routing
        D. forming   E. smoothing

31. A novel in which one or more characters are based on real 31. ___
    people but are given fictitious names is often referred to
    as a
        A. biograph   B. roman à clef   Gothic novel
        D. petit roman   E. roman du roi

32. An award presented for originality shown in devising new 32. ___
    and improved methods in library technology is called the
    _____ medal.
        A. Robinson   B. Caldecott   C. Newbery   D. ALA
        E. Roberts

33. The classification of books relative to their positions on 33. ___
    shelves is usually referred to as _____ classification.
        A. bibliographic   B. Sears   C. Dewey
        D. Library of Congress   E. rigid

34. Another common name for a memorial volume is 34. ___
        A. festschrift   B. memoirs   C. special edition
        D. limited edition   E. tome

35. A computerized service developed by the National Library 35. ___
    of Medicine in 1971 for rapid bibliographic searching of
    current medical literature is called
        A. Medfacts   B. Medservice   C. Medlam   D. Medline
        E. Medfast

36. A work that has been abridged or summarized from some 36. ___
    larger work is usually referred to as a(an)
        A. epithet   B. epitome   C. entropy   D. adaptation
        E. adoption

37. ERIC is an acronym for 37. ___
        A. Educational Research Instruction Center
        B. Educational Resources Informing Center
        C. Educational Resources Information Center
        D. Educational Resources Instruction Center
        E. Educational Research Incentive Center

38. The attributing of false names to authors of books is called 38. ___
        A. plagiarism   B. pseudepigraph   C. pronephros
        D. pseudomorphism   E. preconization

39. A geographical dictionary is usually called a(n) 39. ___
        A. Michelin guide   B. travel guide   C. atlas
        D. guidebook   E. gazetteer

40. Dictionaries devoted to specialized fields, occupations, or 40. ___
    professions are generally referred to as _____ dictionar-
    ies.
        A. encyclopedia   B. usage   C. subject
        D. multi-purpose   E. special

4

41. A manuscript in book form is called a   41. ___
    A. code   B. codex   C. codicil   D. chrestomathy
    E. coda

42. The inscription, used especially in the 15th and 16th cen- 42. ___
    turies, which the printer placed at the end of a manuscript
    or book with facts about its production, author, date, title,
    etc., is called a(n)
    A. colophon   B. summit   C. collating mark
    D. stamp   E. emblem

43. An alphabetical index of words showing the places in the   43. ___
    text of a book where each may be found is called a
    A. configuration   B. colporteur
    C. continuation order   D. concordance
    E. conversion

44. Copies of a newly published book placed in specified li-   44. ___
    braries are designated as _____ copies.
    A. assigned   B. deposit   C. reference
    D. honor   E. circulating

45. Material of transitory interest or value is usually re-   45. ___
    ferred to as
    A. ephemeral   B. epicene   C. ephoral
    D. epicurean   E. epicyclic

46. Errors discovered in a book after printing are usually   46. ___
    called
    A. eccentrics   B. espials   C. escheats
    D. eschewals   E. errata

47. The Latin phrase "ex libris" designates the   47. ___
    A. author   B. title   C. publisher   D. library
    E. distributor

48. A reprint edition of several works of an author is called   48. ___
    a(n)
    A. omnibus book   B. festschrift   C. memorial edition
    D. limited edition   E. special edition

49. A separate printing or reprint of an article or chapter   49. ___
    which has appeared first in a magazine or some other larger
    work is usually called a(n)
    A. special edition   B. offprint   C. limited edition
    D. processed copy   E. detached copy

50. In a card catalog or index, the entry under which full   50. ___
    information is given is called the
    A. secondary entry   B. collation   C. prime entry
    D. main entry   E. tracing

5

KEY (CORRECT ANSWERS)

1.	C	11.	C	21.	E	31.	B	41.	B
2.	A	12.	E	22.	D	32.	A	42.	A
3.	B	13.	D	23.	B	33.	E	43.	D
4.	D	14.	B	24.	B	34.	A	44.	B
5.	C	15.	D	25.	B	35.	D	45.	A
6.	E	16.	A	26.	C	36.	B	46.	E
7.	C	17.	E	27.	D	37.	C	47.	D
8.	D	18.	B	28.	C	38.	B	48.	A
9.	D	19.	E	29.	D	39.	E	49.	B
10.	D	20.	C	30.	B	40.	C	50.	D

EXAMINATION SECTION

TEST 1

DIRECTIONS: Each question or incomplete statement is followed by several suggested answers or completions. Select the one that BEST answers the question or completes the statement. *PRINT THE LETTER OF THE CORRECT ANSWER IN THE SPACE AT THE RIGHT.*

1. The items in a bibliography are arranged in   1.___
   A. alphabetical order according to the author's last name
   B. chronological order according to date of publication
   C. alphabetical order according to the first word in the title
   D. alphabetical order according to name of publisher

2. Which reference source would contain the MOST complete   2.___
   information on the British game of cricket?
   A. THE WORLD ALMANAC
   B. SKEAT'S ETYMOLOGICAL DICTIONARY
   C. READERS' GUIDE TO PERIODICAL LITERATURE
   D. ENCYCLOPEDIA BRITANNICA

3. How are novels arranged on a library shelf?   3.___
   A. Alphabetically by subject
   B. Alphabetically by author's last name
   C. Numerically by Dewey Decimal number
   D. Alphabetically by title

4. In the card catalog, cross reference cards are used   4.___
   PRIMARILY to
   A. locate a book on the shelves
   B. determine the author of a certain work
   C. locate additional information on a subject
   D. find other books by an author

5. Which would NOT be likely to appear on the editorial   5.___
   page of a newspaper?
   A. Readers' reactions   B. Masthead
   C. Syndicated columns   D. Classified ads

Questions 6-10.

DIRECTIONS: Questions 6 through 10 are based on the entry below
from the READERS' GUIDE TO PERIODICAL LITERATURE.
For each question, select the word or expression
that BEST completes the statement or answers the
question, and write its letter in the space at the
right.

LITERARY prizes
Added attraction; Seal Novel Awards for a first novel by a
Canadian. P.S. Nathan. Pub W 216:26 D 3 '79
Case of the two first novels: the Hemingway Award reexamined.
S. Dong. Pub W 215:40+ Je 25 '79
Consolation Prize; awarding of the Austrian State Prize for
Literature to S. de Beauvoir. E. M. von Kuehnelt-Leddihn.
Nat R 31:1040 Ag 17 '79
Hasen wins Hemingway Award; figures suggest 1979 rise in
published first novels. S. Dong. Pub W 215:17-18 Je 11 '79
National Jewish Book Awards. Pub W 215:17 Je 11 '79
1978: the year in review; literary prizes and awards.
il Pub W 215:47-52 F 19 '79
Tenth anniversary of the Freedley Memorial Award. D. B. Wilmeth.
USA Today 108:66 Jl '79
Three groups found awards for African heritage books.
M. Reuter. Pub W 215:26+ Ap 2 '79
   See also
American Book Awards
Carey-Thomas Awards
National Book Awards
National Book Critics Circle Awards
Nobel prizes
Poetry - Awards
Pulitzer prizes
Scientific literature for children - Awards

6. In this entry on literary prizes, how are authors' names   6.___
given?
A. Last name only
B. Last name and then first name
C. First name and then last name
D. Initials and then last name

7. According to this entry on literary prizes, which   7.___
abbreviation does READERS' GUIDE use for *June*?
A. J   B. Je   C. Jn   D. Ju

8. Under the heading *Literary prizes*, the entry *1978: the*   8.___
year in review is listed
A. chronologically   B. alphabetically
C. by subject   D. by degree of importance

9. In the entry titled *Three groups found awards for*
African heritage books, Ap 2 '79 refers to the date the
    A. magazine was published   B. award was given
    C. article was written   D. groups established the award
9.___

10. Which other article appears in the same issue of
PUBLISHERS WEEKLY as *Hasen Wins Hemingway Award*?
    A. Added attraction
    B. Case of the two first novels
    C. National Jewish Book Awards
    D. 1978: the year in review
10.___

Questions 11-25.

DIRECTIONS: Listed below are some types of information you might
want to locate together with several books in which
you might look. For each write the letter of the
BEST answer in the space at the right.

11. The officers and addresses of the regional and district
officers of the Office of Price Administration may be
found in
    A. CONGRESSIONAL DIRECTORY
    B. ENCYCLOPEDIA AMERICANA
    C. STATESMAN'S YEARBOOK
    D. GOVERNMENT MANUAL
    E. LARNED'S NEW HISTORY FOR READY REFERENCE
11.___

12. The current membership of the standing committees of the
Senate may be found in
    A. ENCYCLOPEDIA AMERICANA
    B. CONGRESSIONAL DIRECTORY
    C. WORLD ALMANAC
    D. GOVERNMENTAL MANUAL
    E. STATESMAN'S YEARBOOK
12.___

13. The Washington addresses of the members of Congress may
be found in
    A. WORLD ALMANAC   B. ENCYCLOPEDIA AMERICANA
    C. CONGRESSIONAL DIRECTORY D. GOVERNMENT MANUAL
    E. STATESMAN'S YEARBOOK
13.___

14. To locate summaries of Franklin D. Roosevelt's speeches
in 1942, one should consult
    A. WORLD ALMANAC   B. ENCYCLOPEDIA AMERICANA
    C. READERS' GUIDE   D. CURRENT BIOGRAPHY
    E. WHO'S WHO IN AMERICA
14.___

15. The definition of *Grossmann's law* may be found in Webster's
NEW INTERNATIONAL DICTIONARY in
    A. new words section
    B. below the line in the main alphabet
    C. main alphabet
    D. Gazetteer
    E. biographical dictionary
15.___

16. The provisions and benefits of the New Zealand Social
    Security legislation of 1938 may be found in
        A. STATESMAN'S YEARBOOK
        B. LARNED'S NEW HISTORY FOR READY REFERENCE
        C. ENCYCLOPEDIA AMERICANA
        D. WORLD ALMANAC
        E. GOVERNMENT MANUAL   16.___

17. To find the location of the poem THE HIGHWAYMAN by
    Alfred Noyes, one would look in
        A. BARTLETT'S FAMILIAR QUOTATIONS
        B. COMPTON'S PICTURED ENCYCLOPEDIA
        C. ENCYCLOPEDIA AMERICANA
        D. THE WORLD BOOK
        E. GRANGER'S INDEX TO POETRY AND RECITATIONS   17.___

18. The biography of the Prime Minister of Great Britain may
    be found in
        A. WHO'S WHO IN AMERICA
        B. GRANGER'S INDEX TO POETRY AND RECITATIONS
        C. CURRENT BIOGRAPHY
        D. GROVE'S DICTIONARY OF MUSIC AND MUSICIANS   18.___

19. An account of Antarctic exploration featuring excerpts
    from scientific books and journals:
        A. LARNED'S NEW HISTORY FOR READY REFERENCE
        B. ENCYCLOPEDIA AMERICANA
        C. STATESMAN'S YEARBOOK
        D. GOVERNMENT MANUAL
        E. WORLD ALMANAC   19.___

20. The dates of Ash Wednesday and Easter Sunday from the
    year 1801 through 2000 may be found in
        A. COMPTON'S PICTURED ENCYCLOPEDIA
        B. LARNED'S NEW HISTORY FOR READY REFERENCE
        C. NEW INTERNATIONAL DICTIONARY
        D. WORLD ALMANAC
        E. STATESMAN'S YEARBOOK   20.___

21. The meaning of the letters D.A.G. may be found in the
    NEW STANDARD DICTIONARY in
        A. Key to abbreviations
        B. Statistics of population
        C. main alphabet
        D. Foreign words and phrases
        E. disputed pronunciations   21.___

22. To find the author of the poem beginning *"Thou are not
    lovelier than lilacs"*, look in
        A. GRANGER'S INDEX TO POETRY AND RECITATIONS
        B. COMPTON'S PICTURED ENCYCLOPEDIA
        C. BARTLETT'S FAMILIAR QUOTATIONS
        D. THE WORLD BOOK
        E. ENCYCLOPEDIA AMERICANA   22.___

23. The BOSTON MASSACRE may be found in WEBSTER'S NEW   23.___
INTERNATIONAL DICTIONARY 2ND ED. in the
    A. main alphabet
    B. Gazetteer
    C. new words section
    D. main alphabet below the line
    E. biographical dictionary

24. A table showing the rank in population of the largest   24.___
cities of the United States is the
    A. GOVERNMENT MANUAL
    B. CONGRESSIONAL DICTIONARY
    C. WORLD ALMANAC
    D. WEBSTER'S NEW INTERNATIONAL DICTIONARY

25. The definition of *coup d'etat* may be found in WEBSTER'S 25.___
NEW INTERNATIONAL DICTIONARY in the
    A. Gazetteer
    B. new words
    C. pronouncing biographical dictionary
    D. WORLD ALMANAC
    E. main alphabet

KEY (CORRECT ANSWERS)

1. A		11. D	
2. D		12. B	
3. B		13. C	
4. C		14. C	
5. D		15. C	
6. D		16. A	
7. B		17. E	
8. B		18. C	
9. A		19. A	
10. C		20. D	

21. C
22. A
23. A
24. C
25. E

TEST 2

Questions 1-10.

DIRECTIONS: Listed below are some of the main headings of the
Dewey decimal classification such as might appear
on the library book shelves. Below the headings
are ten topics on which you might want information.
If you know under which heading each topic belongs,
you could go *directly* to the shelf for the book you
want. In the space at the right of each topic, write
the number of the heading that BEST covers the topic.
Use ONE number only for each topic and use *no* number
more than once.

220	Bible	640	Home economics
290	Non-Christian religion	720	Architecture
320	Political science	730	Sculpture
330	Economics	750	Painting
350	Administration	760	Engraving
390	Customs and folklore	770	Photography
530	Physics	780	Music
540	Chemistry	800	Literature
550	Geology	910	Geography
580	Botany	913	Archaeology
590	Zoology	930	Ancient history
620	Engineering	942	English history
630	Agriculture	970	North American history

1. Hunting with a camera   1.____

2. Interior decoration   2.____

3. Excavations in the pyramids   3.____

4. A survey predicting the probability of oil   4.____

5. The poems of Robert Browning   5.____

6. The spread of representative government   6.____

7. A discussion of longitude and latitude   7.____

8. Classification of plants   8.____

9. A discussion of the technical points of bridge building   9.____

10. A copy of the picture, Mona Lisa, by Leonardo da Vinci   10.____

Questions 11-25.

DIRECTIONS: Each of the following statements lists a topic on which you might wish to find a book, together with the *possible* word under which to look for it in the card catalog. For each, write the letter of the BEST answer in the space at the right.

11. French revolution   11.___
    A. Napoleonic wars   B. Reign of terror
    C. France - Revolution   D. Revolution, French
    E. Terror, Reign of

12. North American Indians   12.___
    A. Indians of North America
    B. Aborigines
    C. American aborigines
    D. American Indians
    E. Mounds and mound builders

13. Democracy   13.___
    A. Democracy   B. Free institutions
    C. Popular government   D. Federal government
    E. Politics

14. Soap carving   14.___
    A. Sculpture   B. Soap sculpture
    C. Arts and crafts   D. Fine Arts
    E. Handicrafts

15. Business depressions   15.___
    A. Business cycles   B. Economic cycles
    C. Stabilization in industry D. Economic conditions
    E. Depressions, Business

16. Applied art   16.___
    A. Art industry and trade   B. Decorative arts
    C. Industrial arts   D. Arts and crafts movement
    E. Commercial art

17. Prehistoric antiquities   17.___
    A. Antiquities
    B. Excavations
    C. Lake dwellers and lake dwellings
    D. Archaeology
    E. Ruins

18. Conduits   18.___
    A. Aqueducts   B. Water conduits
    C. Civil engineering   D. Hydraulic engineering
    E. Water supply

19. Actresses   19.___
    A. Actors and actresses   B. Drama
    C. Theater   D. Stage
    E. Acting

20. Abolition of slavery
    A. American history
    C. Civil war
    E. Negroes
    B. Southern states
    D. Slavery
    20.___

21. The 1984 platforms of both the Republican and Democratic
    political parties may be found in
    A. GOVERNMENT MANUAL   B. CURRENT BIOGRAPHY
    C. ENCYCLOPEDIA AMERICANA D. LINCOLN LIBRARY
    E. WORLD ALMANAC
    21.___

22. An authoritative bibliography for each country described
    is given in the
    A. WORLD ALMANAC   B. GOVERNMENT MANUAL
    C. STATESMAN'S YEARBOOK D. CONGRESSIONAL DIRECTORY
    E. CURRENT BIOGRAPHY
    22.___

23. To find the author and title of the poem beginning *"Dear
    charming, nymph, neglected and decried"*, look in
    A. COMPTON'S PICTURED ENCYCLOPEDIA
    B. BARTLETT'S FAMILIAR QUOTATIONS
    C. GRANGER'S INDEX TO POETRY AND RECITATION
    D. THE WORLD BOOK
    E. ENCYCLOPEDIA AMERICANA
    23.___

24. A history of Alaska told by quotations (excerpts) from the
    writings of several historians may be found in
    A. STATESMAN'S YEARBOOK
    B. ENCYCLOPEDIA AMERICANA
    C. LARNED'S NEW HISTORY FOR READY REFERENCE
    D. WORLD ALMANAC
    E. CONGRESSIONAL DIRECTORY
    24.___

25. A biographical note on Jane Addams may be found in the
    NEW STANDARD DICTIONARY in the
    A. main alphabet
    B. foreign words and phrases
    C. biographical section
    D. statistics of population
    E. rules for simplification of spelling
    25.___

KEY (CORRECT ANSWERS)

1. 770
2. 640
3. 913
4. 550
5. 800

6. 320
7. 910
8. 580
9. 620
10. 750

11. C
12. A
13. A
14. B
15. A

16. A
17. D
18. A
19. A
20. D

21. E
22. C
23. C
24. C
25. A

TEST 3

Questions 1-20.

DIRECTIONS: Each question consists of a statement. You are to indicate whether the statement is TRUE (T) or FALSE (F). *PRINT THE LETTER OF THE CORRECT ANSWER IN THE SPACE AT THE RIGHT.*

1. Biographies of poets may be found in GRANGER'S INDEX TO POETRY AND RECITATIONS.   1.____

2. To use THE LINCOLN LIBRARY OF ESSENTIAL INFORMATION, one should consult the index.   2.____

3. The words at the top of each page in the dictionary indicate the inclusive contents of the page.   3.____

4. THE STATESMAN'S YEARBOOK is published biennially.   4.____

5. The index is a valuable aid in the use of the ENCYCLOPAEDIA BRITANNICA.   5.____

6. The arrangement of BARTLETT'S FAMILIAR QUOTATIONS is chronological by author.   6.____

7. CURRENT BIOGRAPHY is arranged alphabetically.   7.____

8. The ENCYCLOPEDIA AMERICANA is arranged in large subject groups with an index.   8.____

9. WEBSTER'S NEW INTERNATIONAL DICTIONARY arranges all kinds of words in the English language in one alphabetical list.   9.____

10. Names of government officials may be found in the U.S. GOVERNMENT MANUAL.   10.____

11. WHO'S WHO IN AMERICA contains biographies of important people both living and dead.   11.____

12. COMPTON'S PICTURED ENCYCLOPEDIA is particularly good for children in the intermediate grades.   12.____

13. The articles in both the ENCYCLOPEDIA BRITANNICA and the ENCYCLOPEDIA AMERICANA are signed.   13.____

14. A feature of the NEW STANDARD DICTIONARY is the divided page by which obsolete words are given below the line.   14.____

15. The U.S. GOVERNMENT MANUAL contains biographies of government officials.   15.____

16. BARTLETT'S FAMILIAR QUOTATIONS contains complete poems.   16.___

17. CURRENT BIOGRAPHY is published monthly and then cumulated.   17.___

18. CURRENT BIOGRAPHY contains biographies of persons in the news.   18.___

19. A description of the duties of the departments of the United States government will be found in the GOVERNMENT MANUAL.   19.___

20. An encyclopedia should be consulted for the pronunciation of words.   20.___

Questions 21-25.

DIRECTIONS: Listed below are some types of information you might want to locate, together with several books in which you might look. For each, write the letter of the BEST answer in the space at the right.

21. To find a list of magazine articles published in 1919 on the Versailles Treaty, you would consult   21.___
    A. the ENCYCLOPAEDIA BRITANNICA
    B. THE READER'S GUIDE
    C. LARNED'S NEW HISTORY FOR READY REFERENCE
    D. the card catalog
    E. WEBSTER'S NEW INTERNATIONAL DICTIONARY

22. The purposes, powers, and personnel of the United States Government War Agencies of World War II may be found in the   22.___
    A. CONGRESSIONAL DIRECTORY   B. GOVERNMENT MANUAL
    C. STATESMAN'S YEARBOOK   D. ENCYCLOPAEDIA BRITANNICA
    E. WORLD ALMANAC

23. A list of representative publications of departments and agencies of the federal government may be found in   23.___
    A. LARNED'S NEW HISTORY FOR READY REFERENCE
    B. STATESMAN'S YEARBOOK
    C. GOVERNMENT MANUAL
    D. AMERICAN ENCYCLOPEDIA
    E. CONGRESSIONAL DIRECTORY

24. For a discussion of the life and works of Beethoven, one should consult   24.___
    A. CURRENT BIOGRAPHY
    B. a daily newspaper
    C. GRANGER'S INDEX TO POETRY AND RECITATIONS
    D. GROVE'S DICTIONARY OF MUSIC AND MUSICIANS
    E. WHO'S WHO

25. The population of Topeka, Kansas, may be found in the   25.___
    NEW STANDARD DICTIONARY in the
        A. main alphabet
        B. foreign words and phrases
        C. disputed pronunciations
        D. key to abbreviations
        E. statistics of population

_____

KEY (CORRECT ANSWERS)

1. F		11. F
2. T		12. T
3. T		13. T
4. F		14. F
5. T		15. F
6. T		16. F
7. T		17. T
8. F		18. T
9. F		19. T
10. T		20. F

21. B
22. B
23. C
24. D
25. E

_____

EXAMINATION SECTION

TEST 1

DIRECTIONS: Each question or incomplete statement is followed by
several suggested answers or completions. Select the
one that BEST answers the question or completes the
statement. *PRINT THE LETTER OF THE CORRECT ANSWER IN
THE SPACE AT THE RIGHT.*

Questions 1-16.

DIRECTIONS: Choose the CORRECT reference source for each.
Indicate the correct letter in the space at the
right.

1. Maps showing the congressional districts of the states   1.____
    may be found in the
        A. GOVERNMENT MANUAL   B. STATESMAN'S YEARBOOK
        C. CONGRESSIONAL DIRECTORY   D. WORLD ALMANAC
        E. ENCYCLOPEDIA AMERICANA

2. A list of presidents of the Argentine Republic from 1898   2.____
    to 1988 may be found in the
        A. LARNED'S NEW HISTORY FOR READY REFERENCE
        B. ENCYCLOPEDIA AMERICANA
        C. GOVERNMENT MANUAL
        D. WORLD ALMANAC
        E. STATESMAN'S YEARBOOK

3. To find the author and location of the poem whose title   3.____
    is THE LOTUS EATERS, one would look in
        A. READERS' GUIDE
        B. GRANGER'S INDEX TO POETRY AND RECITATIONS
        C. BARTLETT'S FAMILIAR QUOTATIONS
        D. ENCYCLOPEDIA AMERICANA
        E. GROVE'S DICTIONARY OF MUSIC AND MUSICIANS

4. Brief biographies of members of Congress may be found   4.____
    in the
        A. ENCYCLOPEDIA AMERICANA   B. CONGRESSIONAL DIRECTORY
        C. WORLD ALMANAC   D. U.S. GOVERNMENT MANUAL
        E. STATESMAN'S YEARBOOK

5. To locate the poem whose title is SONG OF THE CAMELS by   5.____
    Elizabeth Coatsworth, look in the
        A. READERS' GUIDE
        B. BARTLETT'S FAMILIAR QUOTATIONS
        C. GRANGER'S INDEX TO POETRY AND RECITATIONS
        D. THE WORLD BOOK
        E. ENCYCLOPEDIA AMERICANA

6. An article on international arbitration from ancient   6. ___
   to modern times may be found in the
   A. WORLD ALMANAC
   B. STATESMAN'S YEARBOOK
   C. GOVERNMENT MANUAL
   D. LARNED'S NEW HISTORY FOR READY REFERENCE
   E. CONGRESSIONAL DIRECTORY

7. Statistics showing the production of raw sugar for the   7. ___
   years 1970 through 1988 may be found in the
   A. STATESMAN'S YEARBOOK
   B. LARNED'S NEW HISTORY FOR READY REFERENCE
   C. WORLD ALMANAC
   D. LINCOLN LIBRARY
   E. READERS' GUIDE

8. The meaning of *capitis diminutio* may be found in THE NEW   8. ___
   STANDARD DICTIONARY in the
   A. statistics of population
   B. foreign words and phrases
   C. key to abbreviations
   D. main alphabet
   E. Gazetteer

9. The definition of N I R A may be found in WEBSTER'S NEW   9. ___
   INTERNATIONAL DICTIONARY in the
   A. main alphabet
   B. pronouncing biographical dictionary
   C. arbitrary signs and symbols
   D. abbreviations
   E. Gazetteer

10. For a description of the musical instrument pianoforte,   10. ___
    one should consult the
    A. WORLD ALMANAC
    B. GROVE'S DICTIONARY OF MUSIC AND MUSICIANS
    C. GRANGER'S INDEX TO POETRY AND RECITATIONS
    D. BARTLETT'S FAMILIAR QUOTATIONS
    E. READERS' GUIDE

11. For a map of Oceana, one should consult the   11. ___
    A. RAND-MCNALLY ATLAS
    B. STATESMAN'S YEARBOOK
    C. geography textbook
    D. NATIONAL GEOGRAPHIC MAGAZINE
    E. NEW STANDARD DICTIONARY

12. For information about Russia with pictures of Russian   12. ___
    life, one should consult
    A. STATESMAN'S YEARBOOK
    B. WORLD ALMANAC
    C. COMPTON'S PICTURED ENCYCLOPEDIA
    D. NEW STANDARD DICTIONARY
    E. the librarian

13. The election returns by states may be found in   13.___
    A. WORLD ALMANAC   B. GOVERNMENT MANUAL
    C. ENCYCLOPEDIA AMERICANA   D. STATESMAN'S YEARBOOK
    E. CONGRESSIONAL DIRECTORY

14. To locate the poem whose first line is *"By none but me*   14.___
can the tale be told", one should look in
    A. BARTLETT'S FAMILIAR QUOTATIONS
    B. READERS' GUIDE
    C. LINCOLN LIBRARY OF ESSENTIAL INFORMATION
    D. GRANGER'S INDEX TO POETRY AND RECITATIONS
    E. GROVE'S DICTIONARY OF MUSIC AND MUSICIANS

15. A list of well-known educators showing birth dates may   15.___
be found in
    A. LINCOLN LIBRARY OF ESSENTIAL INFORMATION
    B. WORLD ALMANAC
    C. CURRENT BIOGRAPHY
    D. WHO'S WHO IN AMERICA
    E. ENCYCLOPEDIA AMERICANA

16. The location of Coffin Island may be found in the NEW   16.___
STANDARD DICTIONARY in
    A. main alphabet
    B. biographical section
    C. statistics of population
    D. foreign words and phrases
    E. key to abbreviations

Questions 17-19.

DIRECTIONS: In Questions 17 to 19, choose the CORRECT subject
              under which the topic should be referenced.

17. Labor strikes   17.___
    A. Conciliation, Industrial
    B. Industrial relations
    C. Strikes and lock-outs
    D. Labor and laboring classes
    E. Capital and labor

18. Fashions   18.___
    A. Style in dress   B. Clothing and dress
    C. Fashion   D. Costume
    E. Dressmaking

19. Delinquent children   19.___
    A. Crime and criminals
    B. Juvenile delinquency
    C. Delinquency, Juvenile
    D. Reformatories
    E. Defective and delinquent classes

Questions 20-23.

DIRECTIONS: Each question consists of a statement. You are to
               indicate whether the statement is TRUE (T) or FALSE (F).
               *PRINT THE LETTER OF THE CORRECT ANSWER IN THE SPACE AT
               THE RIGHT.*

20.   Complete poems are printed in GRANGER'S INDEX TO   20.____
      POETRY AND RECITATIONS.

21.   A biography of the painter Murillo may be found in   21.____
      GROVE'S DICTIONARY OF MUSIC AND MUSICIANS.

22.   A key to the abbreviations of the names of magazines   22.____
      used in the READERS' GUIDE is given in the front of each
      issue.

23.   The STATESMAN'S YEARBOOK contains no information on   23.____
      commerce.

24.   The longest rivers in tne world may be *most easily* found   24.____
      in the
            A. ENCYCLOPEDIA BRITTANICA
            B. LIBRARY JOURNAL
            C. WORLD ALMANAC
            D. INTERNATIONAL GEOPHYSICAL YEARBOOK

25.   The list of American president's can be *most easily* found   25.____
      in the
            A. READERS GUIDE   B. WORLD ALMANAC
            C. RAND McNALLY ATLAS   D. WARREN COMMISSION REPORT

                              ____

KEY (CORRECT ANSWERS)

1. C	11. A
2. E	12. C
3. B	13. A
4. B	14. D
5. C	15. D
6. D	16. A
7. C	17. C
8. B	18. C
9. D	19. B
10. B	20. F

21. F
22. T
23. F
24. C
25. B

TEST 2

Questions 1-14.

DIRECTIONS: Each question consists of a statement. You are to indicate whether the statement is TRUE (T) or FALSE (F). *PRINT THE LETTER OF THE CORRECT ANSWER IN THE SPACE AT THE RIGHT.*

1. There are author cards in the catalog for every writer who has books in the library.   1.___

2. The labels on the outside of the catalog drawers indicate the part of the alphabet which is included in each drawer.   2.___

3. The articles *a*, *an*, and *the* are disregarded except when they occur at the beginning of titles.   3.___

4. Fiction books do not usually have Dewey Decimal classification numbers.   4.___

5. A card for a book about Edgar Allan Poe will be filed in front of a card for a book by Edgar Allan Poe.   5.___

6. Cards in the dictionary card catalog are filed in straight alphabetical order.   6.___

7. The card catalog gives information as to date of publication of a book.   7.___

8. Abbreviations in titles, names, etc. are usually regarded as if spelled in full when they need to be considered in the alphabetical arrangement in the card catalog.   8.___

9. The *see also* cross reference card is an aid to further reading on a subject.   9.___

10. Books by Mark Twain will be found under Twain (pen name) and Clemens, a real name.   10.___

11. Library books are arranged on the shelves according to size.   11.___

12. For individual biographies and autobiographies, some libraries use B instead of a number.   12.___

13. Most non-fiction books have at least three cards in the card catalog.   13.___

14. A card saying *Exports see Commerce* means that there is no material in the library on *Exports*.   14.___

Questions 15-25.

DIRECTIONS: In Column II are some common library terms. In
               Column I are definitions for those terms. Match
               the terms to the definitions by placing the letter
               for the term in the space at the right of the
               corresponding definition.

COLUMN I

COLUMN II

15. That part of a book's call
    number which represents the
    author's name

A. Author number   15.___

B. Binding

16. Reference made from one part
    of a book or card catalog to
    another where the same or
    allied subject is treated

C. Call number   16.___

D. Class numbers

E. Cross reference

17. Refers from word not used
    to another

F. Open entry   17.___

18. List of books as they
    stand on the shelves

G. Pseudonym   18.___

H. Secondary entry

19. The combination of numbers
    which indicate the location
    of a library book

I. See reference   19.___

J. Shelf list

20. Author's pen name

K. Subject analytic   20.___

21. That part of a call
    number which indicates
    the subject of a book

L. Subject card   21.___

22. Subject card for a part
    of the book   22.___

23. The cover of a book   23.___

24. An entry for a serial which
    has not ceased publication   24.___

25. A card with the subject
    heading printed or typed
    on the top line   25.___

———

KEY (CORRECT ANSWERS)

1. T	11. F
2. T	12. T
3. F	13. T
4. T	14. F
5. F	15. A
6. F	16. E
7. T	17. I
8. T	18. J
9. T	19. C
10. F	20. G

21. D
22. K
23. B
24. F
25. L

———

TEST 3

Questions 1-10.

DIRECTIONS: Listed below are some of the main headings of the
Dewey Decimal classification such as might appear
on the library book shelves. Below the headings
are ten topics on which you might want information.
If you know under which heading each topic belongs,
you could go directly to the shelf for the book you
want. In the space at the right of each topic,
write the number of the heading that BEST covers
the topic. Use *one* number only for each topic and
use no number more than once.

220	Bible	640	Home economics
290	Non-Christian religion	720	Architecture
320	Political science	730	Sculpture
330	Economics	750	Painting
350	Administration	760	Engraving
390	Customs and folklore	770	Photography
530	Physics	780	Music
540	Chemistry	800	Literature
550	Geology	910	Geography
580	Botany	913	Archaeology
590	Zoology	930	Ancient history
620	Engineering	942	English history
630	Agriculture	970	North American history

1.   The westward expansion of the United States   1._____

2.   Theories of money   2._____

3.   Gothic building   3._____

4.   Cookery   4._____

5.   The growth of the ancient Roman Empire   5._____

6.   The Restoration period in England   6._____

7.   The opera FAUST   7._____

8.   Soy beans   8._____

9.   A commentary on the Bible   9._____

10.   Myths of Greece and Rome   10._____

Questions 11-25.

DIRECTIONS: Each question consists of a statement. You are to
indicate whether the statement is TRUE (T) or FALSE (F).
*PRINT THE LETTER OF THE CORRECT ANSWER IN THE SPACE AT
THE RIGHT.*

11.   The title page date and the copyright date give the same   11.____
information about a book.

12.   The appendix of a book contains additional material not   12.____
included in the text of a book.

13.   Fiction books *rarely* have indexes.   13.____

14.   The publisher of a book is the person who has written it.   14.____

15.   The preface of a book should be read because it is the   15.____
MOST interesting part of the book.

16.   The table of contents is *usually* an alphabetical list   16.____
of the topics treated in the book, telling where to find
each one.

17.   A footnote may either explain a statement in the text of   17.____
the book or it may cite an authority for the statement.

18.   The index is the key to the book and should be used in   18.____
looking up a single point or fact.

19.   The author's outline of his book might be found in the   19.____
index.

20.   The preface explains the purpose of the book.   20.____

21.   To judge the scope of a book, consult the table of   21.____
contents.

22.   A *definite* citation to an authority for a statement made   22.____
in the text is given in the appendix.

23.   The full name of the publisher is ALWAYS found on the   23.____
cover of the book.

24.   The preface lists *all* the important topics and names   24.____
terms which are discussed in a book in strict alphabetical
order.

25.   The bibliography is a list of books for further reading.   25.____

———

KEY (CORRECT ANSWERS)

1.	970		11.	F
2.	330		12.	T
3.	720		13.	T
4.	640		14.	F
5.	930		15.	F
6.	942		16.	F
7.	780		17.	T
8.	630		18.	T
9.	220		19.	F
10.	290		20.	T

21.	T
22.	F
23.	F
24.	F
25.	T

TEST 4

Questions 1-15.

DIRECTIONS: Each question consists of a statement. You are to indicate whether the statement is TRUE (T) or FALSE (F). *PRINT THE LETTER OF THE CORRECT ANSWER IN THE SPACE AT THE RIGHT.*

1. There are author cards in the catalog for *every* writer who has books in the library.   1.___

2. A card reading *Forging see also Blacksmithing* means that there is additional material under the heading *Blacksmithing*.   2.___

3. Books on Botany will be found in the 900's in the Dewey decimal classification.   3.___

4. Books by O. Henry will be entered under both O. Henry and his real name, William Sydney Porter.   4.___

5. An analytic card describes a part of a book.   5.___

6. The card catalog shows the books in a library as they stand on the shelves.   6.___

7. Subject cards are easily distinguished in the card catalog because the first line is typed either in red or in full black capitals.   7.___

8. The usual alphabetical arrangement for the dictionary card catalog is letter by letter to the end of a word and then word by word.   8.___

9. Books of biography are alphabetized by the author's name on the shelves.   9.___

10. The cards in the library catalog are arranged according to the call numbers of the books they represent.   10.___

11. The articles *a*, *an*, and *the* are disregarded except when they occur at the beginning of titles.   11.___

12. Most non-fiction books have AT LEAST three cards in the card catalog.   12.___

13. For individual biographies and autobiographies, some libraries use B instead of a number.   13.___

14. A card for a book about Edgar Allan Poe will be filed   14. ____
in front of a card for a book by Edgar Allan Poe.

15. Abbreviations in titles, names, etc. are *usually* regarded   15. ____
as if spelled in full when they need to be considered in
the alphabetical arrangement in the card catalog.

Questions 16-25.

DIRECTIONS: Below you will find the titles or descriptions of
books with a list of possible words under which you
would find each in the card catalog. For each,
write the letter of the BEST answer in the space at
the right.

16. The call number for a book entitled GIRLS AT WORK IN   16. ____
AVIATION written by Dickey Meyer, a pseudonym for
Georgette Louise (Meyer) Chappelle:
    A. Chappelle   B. Dickey   C. Louise
    D. Georgette   E. Meyer

17. A book entitled HER SON'S WIFE by Dorothea Francis   17. ____
(Canfield) Fisher:
    A. Son's   B. Canfield   C. Francis
    D. Wife   E. Fisher

18. A book by Annie (Wilhelm) Williams-Heller and Josephine   18. ____
(Vercelli) McCarthy entitled SOYBEANS FROM SOUP TO NUTS:
    A. Vercelli   B. Heller   C. Soup
    D. William-Heller   E. Wilhelm

19. A book entitled DEMOCRACY, EFFICIENCY, STABILITY; AN   19. ____
APPRAISAL OF AMERICAN GOVERNMENT:
    A. Stability   B. Government
    C. American government   D. Democracy
    E. Efficiency

20. The book entitled 1001 CHRISTMAS FACTS AND FANCIES: 20. ____
    A. Noa-Pap   B. Cha-Cis   C. Fab-Fas
    D. Aab-Art   E. Fat-Fay

21. A book entitled THE FIGHT FOR LIFE by Paul Henry De   21. ____
Kruif:
    A. Kruif   B. Life   C. De Kruif
    D. Henry   E. Paul

22. A book entitled WITH THE TURKS IN THRACE by Ellis   22. ____
Ashmead-Bartlett:
    A. Bartlett   B. Ellis   C. Ashmead-Bartlett
    D. Turks   E. Thrace

23. A book entitled THE FORGE IN THE FOREST: 23. ____
    A. Forge   B. Blacksmiths
    C. Forests and forestry   D. Forest
    E. Fiction

24. A book by Willard De Mille Price entitled JAPAN RIDES   24.____
 THE TIGER:
    A. Price   B. De Mille   C. Willard
    D. Mille   E. Tiger

25. A book by Seymour Van Santvoord entitled OCTAVIA; A TALE   25.____
 OF ANCIENT ROME:
    A. Seymour   B. Van Santvoord   C. Santvoord
    D. Fiction   E. Ancient history

——

KEY (CORRECT ANSWERS)

1. T		11. F	
2. T		12. T	
3. F		13. T	
4. F		14. F	
5. T		15. T	
6. F		16. A	
7. T		17. E	
8. T		18. D	
9. F		19. D	
10. F		20. A	

21. C
22. C
23. A
24. A
25. B

——

EXAMINATION SECTION

TEST 1

DIRECTIONS: Each question or incomplete statement is followed by several suggested answers or completions. Select the one that BEST answers the question or completes the statement. *PRINT THE LETTER OF THE CORRECT ANSWER IN THE SPACE AT THE RIGHT.*

1. An employee requests a book which is not in the department 1.____
    library.
    Of the following, the MOST advisable course of action for
    you to take is to
    A. attempt to get the book for him by means of the
        department's affiliation with the public library
    B. explain that the book is not available from the
        department's library
    C. suggest that he try his local public library and give
        him a list of local libraries
    D. tell him where he may purchase the book and offer to
        make the purchase for him

2. The catalog for the use of department employees has just 2.____
    been thoroughly checked and revised by a professional
    librarian. After trying to find the name of a book in
    the catalog, an employee tells you that he cannot find
    it.
    Of the following, the MOST advisable action for you to
    take FIRST is to
    A. call the public library for the exact title
    B. look it up in the catalog yourself
    C. look through the stacks for the book
    D. tell him you are sorry but the book is not in the
        department library

3. You find that three pages are missing from one of the 3.____
    copies of a very popular book in the department library.
    Of the following, the MOST advisable action for you to
    take is to
    A. discard the book since its usefulness is now sharply
        curtailed
    B. order another copy of the book but keep the old copy
        until the new one is received
    C. report the fact to the head of the department and
        request further instructions
    D. type copies of the pages from another volume of the
        book and tape them in the appropriate place

4. The department library is scheduled to close at 5 P.M. 4.____
    It is now 4:55, and an employee reading a book shows no
    signs of leaving.
    Of the following, the MOST advisable action for you to
    take is to
    A. tell him it is time to leave
    B. tell him the time and ask him if he wishes to borrow
        the book

C. turn the lights off and on, indirectly suggesting
   that he leave
D. wait until he decides to leave

5. The dealer from whom you have been buying books for the
   department library has informed you that henceforth he
   can give you only a fifteen percent instead of a twenty
   percent discount.
   Of the following, the MOST advisable course of action for
   you to take FIRST is to
       A. accept the fifteen percent discount
       B. inform the head of your department
       C. investigate the discount given by other book dealers
       D. order directly from the publishers

5.___

6. Your supervisor is a professional librarian and is
   responsible for the selection of material to be added to
   the department library in which you are an employee.
   Shortly after you start on the job, an employee of the
   department brings you a written request to have several
   books of his choice added to the library.
   Of the following, the MOST advisable course of action
   for you to take is to
       A. order the books immediately
       B. pass the suggestion along to your supervisor
       C. refuse to accept his suggestion
       D. tell him that he will have to buy the books

6.___

7. You object to your supervisor's plan to change the system
   in the department library from closed to open stacks.
   Of the following, the MOST advisable course of action for
   you to take is to
       A. ask other members of the staff to support your
          objections
       B. await further instructions and then do as you are told
       C. discuss your objections with your supervisor
       D. send a brief report of your objections to the
          department head

7.___

8. Two weeks after you begin working in the department
   library, you learn that books in library bindings last
   twice as long as those with the publishers' bindings.
   Of the following, the MOST advisable course of action for
   you to follow is to
       A. buy only paperbound books
       B. have all new books put in library bindings
       C. put in library bindings only rare editions
       D. put in library bindings only those books likely to
          get hard use

8.___

9. Your superior is away on an official trip. You have been
   asked to type several hundred catalog cards before he
   returns. Just as you begin the job, the typewriter breaks
   down.
   Of the following, the MOST advisable course of action for
   you to take is to

9.___

A. arrange to have the typewriter repaired as soon as
    possible
B. do the cards by hand
C. postpone the job until after your supervisor returns
D. write to your supervisor for advice

10. Your supervisor in the department library is out for the   10.___
    day. You receive a telephone call from another city depart-
    ment asking if they may borrow one of the books in your
    library.
    Of the following, the MOST advisable action for you to take
    FIRST is to tell the department
    A. that books are not permitted out of the department
    B. that you will check and call back the next day
    C. to send a representative to inquire the next day
    D. to write a letter to the department head

11. Two months have passed since the head of the department   11.___
    has borrowed one of the books in the department library.
    Of the following, the MOST advisable action for you to
    take is to
    A. ask the department head if he wishes to keep the
        book out longer
    B. leave a note for the department head telling him
        that the book should be returned immediately
    C. wait another month and then write the book off as
        lost
    D. wait until you receive another request for the book

12. Your supervisor tells you that he would like to have all   12.___
    old book cards replaced, all torn pages mended, and the
    books put in good condition in all other respects by the
    following day. You know that this is an impossible task.
    Of the following, the MOST advisable course of action for
    you to take is to
    A. attempt to finish as much of the job as possible
    B. explain the difficulties involved to the supervisor
        and await further instruction
    C. ignore the request since it is completely unreasonable
    D. make a complaint to the head of the department

13. The library in which you work has received about fifty   13.___
    new books. These books must be cataloged, but you have
    had no experience in this type of work. However, you
    have been told that a professional librarian will join
    the staff in about six weeks.
    Of the following, the MOST advisable course of action for
    you to take in the meantime is to
    A. close the library for a week and try to do the
        cataloging yourself
    B. lend the books only to those who can get special
        permission
    C. let the users take the books even though they are not
        cataloged
    D. put all the books in storage until they can be cataloged

14. The hospital library in which you work has a large back-   14.___
    log of books that need to be mended. You are unable to
    do more than a small part of the job by yourself. One of
    the patients in the hospital has done book binding and
    mending. He offers to help you because he sees the need
    for doing the job and because he wants something to do with
    his hands.
    Of the following, the MOST advisable course of action for
    you to take is to
       A. accept his offer on condition that the doctor approves
       B. ask him to push the book cart around the wards so you
          will be free to do the mending
       C. refuse his offer
       D. write a letter to his former employer to find out
          whether he is a good bookbinder

15. You accidentally spill a glass of water over an open   15.___
    book.
    Of the following, the MOST advisable action for you to
    take FIRST in most cases is to
       A. discard the book to prevent the water from spoiling
          other material
       B. hang the book up by its binding
       C. press the covers together to squeeze out the water
       D. separate the wet pages with blotters

16. In mending a book, you overturn a jar of glue on a new   16.___
    book.
    Of the following, the MOST advisable action for you to
    take FIRST is to
       A. allow the glue to harden so that it may be peeled off
       B. attempt to wipe off the glue with any clean scrap
          paper
       C. discard the book to prevent other materials from being
          spoiled
       D. report the incident immediately to your supervisor

17. Of the following, the situation LEAST likely to result   17.___
    in injury to books is one in which
       A. all books support each other standing upright
       B. short books are placed between tall ones
       C. the books are as close together as possible
       D. the books lean against the sides of the shelves

18. Of the following, a damp cloth may BEST be used to clean   18.___
    a cloth book cover that has been coated with
       A. benzene   B. gold leaf
       C. turpentine   D. varnish

19. Decay of leather bindings may be MOST effectively   19.___
    delayed by
       A. a short tanning period
       B. air conditioning
       C. rubbing periodically with a damp cloth
       D. treatment with heat

20. When paste is used to mend a page, it is MOST desirable   20.___
    that the page should then be
    A. aired   B. heated   C. pressed   D. sprayed

21. A book that is perfectly clean but has been used by   21.___
    someone with chicken pox can probably BEST be handled by
    A. burning, followed by proper disposal of the ashes
    B. forty-eight hour exposure to ultraviolet light
    C. keeping it out of circulation for six months
    D. treating it the same as any other book

22. The BEST combination of temperature and humidity for books   22.___
    is temperature ____ degrees, humidity ____.
    A. 50-60; 20-30%   B. 60-70; 10-20%
    C. 60-70; 50-60%   D. 70-80; 70-80%

23. When a new book is received, it is LEAST important to   23.___
    keep a record of the
    A. author's name
    B. cost of the book
    C. number of pages
    D. source from which it was obtained

24. You have just received from the publisher a new book for   24.___
    the department library, but you find that the binding is
    torn.
    Of the following, the MOST advisable action for you to
    take is to
    A. mend the binding and take no further action
    B. mend the binding but claim a price discount
    C. report the damage to the department head
    D. send the book back to the publisher

25. Of the following, a characteristic of MOST photographic   25.___
    charging systems is that
    A. book cards are not used
    B. charging is done by one person
    C. date due is stamped on borrower's card
    D. transaction cards are not used

_____

KEY (CORRECT ANSWERS)

1. A		11. A	
2. B		12. B	
3. D		13. C	
4. B		14. A	
5. C		15. D	
6. B		16. B	
7. C		17. A	
8. D		18. D	
9. A		19. B	
10. B		20. C	

21. D
22. C
23. C
24. D
25. B

_____

TEST 2

DIRECTIONS: Each question or incomplete statement is followed by several suggested answers or completions. Select the one that BEST answers the question or completes the statement. *PRINT THE LETTER OF THE CORRECT ANSWER IN THE SPACE AT THE RIGHT.*

1. In a card catalog, a reference from one subject heading to   1.___
   another is MOST commonly called a(n) ____ reference.
     A. cross   B. direct   C. primary   D. indirect

2. A book which is shortened by omission of detail but which   2.___
   retains the general sense of the original is called a(n)
     A. compendium   B. manuscript
     C. miniature   D. abridgment

3. An anonymous book is a   3.___
     A. book published before 1500
     B. book whose author is unknown
     C. copy which is defective
     D. work that is out of print

4. All the letters, figures, and symbols assigned to a book   4.___
   to indicate its location on library shelves comprise the
   ____ number.
     A. call   B. Cutter   C. index   D. inventory

5. The term *format* does NOT refer to a book's   5.___
     A. binding   B. size
     C. theme   D. typography

6. The term *card catalog* USUALLY refers to a   6.___
     A. catalog consisting of loose-leaf pages upon which
       the cards are pasted
     B. catalog in which entries are on separate cards
       arranged in a definite order
     C. catalog of the cards available from the Library of
       Congress
     D. record on cards of the works which have been weeded
       out of the library collection

7. The term *circulation record* USUALLY refers to a record of   7.___
     A. daily attendance
     B. the books borrowed
     C. the most popular books
     D. the books out on interlibrary loan

8. Reading shelves USUALLY involves checking the shelves to   8.___
   see that all the books
     A. are in the correct order
     B. are suitable for the library's patrons
     C. are there
     D. have been cataloged correctly

9. In an alphabetical catalog of book titles and authors' names, the name *de Santis* would be filed
    A. after *DeWitt*
    B. after *Sanders*
    C. before AND THEN THERE WERE NONE
    D. before *Deutsch*

9.___

10. In typing catalog cards, the shift key on the typewriter would be used to
    A. change from black ribbon to red ribbon
    B. move the carriage from left to right
    C. move the carriage from right to left
    D. type capitals

10.___

11. The abbreviation e.g. means *most nearly*
    A. as follows   B. for example
    C. refer to   D. that is

11.___

12. The abbreviation ff. means *most nearly*
    A. and following pages   B. formerly
    C. frontispiece   D. the end

12.___

13. The abbreviation ibid. means *most nearly*
    A. consult the index   B. in the same place
    C. see below   D. turn the page

13.___

14. *Ex libris* is a Latin phrase meaning
    A. former librarian   B. from the books
    C. without charge   D. without liberty

14.___

15. An expurgated edition of a book is one which
    A. contains many printing errors
    B. includes undesirable passages
    C. is not permitted in public libraries
    D. omits objectionable material

15.___

16. The re-charging of a book to a borrower is USUALLY called
    A. fining   B. processing
    C. reissue   D. renewal

16.___

17. A sheet of paper that is pierced with holes is
    A. borated   B. collated
    C. perforated   D. serrated

17.___

18. *Glossary* means *most nearly* a(n)
    A. dictionary of selected terms in a particular book or field
    B. list of chapter headings in the order in which they appear in a book
    C. section of the repairing division which coats books with a protective lacquer
    D. alphabetical table of the contents of a book

18.___

19. *Accessioning* means *most nearly*
    A. acquiring books
    B. arranging books for easy access
    C. donating books as gifts
    D. listing books in the order of purchase

19.___

20. *Bookplate* means *most nearly*
    A. a label in a book showing who owns it
    B. a metal device for holding books upright
    C. a rounded zinc surface upon which a page is printed
    D. the flat part of the binding of a book

20.___

21. *Thesaurus* means *most nearly* a book which
    A. contains instructions on how to prepare a thesis
    B. contains words grouped according to similarity of
       meaning
    C. describes the techniques of dramatic acting
    D. gives quotations from well-known works of literature

21.___

22. *Salacious* means *most nearly*
    A. careful   B. delicious   C. lewd   D. salty

22.___

23. *Pseudonym* means *most nearly*
    A. false report   B. fictitious name
    C. libelous statement   D. psychic phenomenon

23.___

24. *Gamut* means *most nearly* a(n)
    A. bookworm   B. simpleton
    C. vagrant   D. entire range

24.___

25. *Monograph* means *most nearly* a
    A. machine for duplicating typewritten material by
       means of a stencil
    B. picture reproduced on an entire page of a manuscript
    C. single chart used to represent statistical data
    D. systematic treatise on a particular subject

25.___

KEY (CORRECT ANSWERS)

1. A		11. B	
2. D		12. A	
3. B		13. B	
4. A		14. B	
5. C		15. D	
6. B		16. D	
7. B		17. C	
8. A		18. A	
9. D		19. D	
10. D		20. A	

21. B
22. C
23. B
24. D
25. D

TEST 3

DIRECTIONS: Each question or incomplete statement is followed by several suggested answers or completions. Select the one that BEST answers the question or completes the statement. *PRINT THE LETTER OF THE CORRECT ANSWER IN THE SPACE AT THE RIGHT.*

Questions 1-15.

DIRECTIONS: Questions 1 through 15 are to be answered SOLELY on the basis of the information contained in the following passage.

Machines may be useful for bibliographic purposes, but they will be useful only if we study the bibliographic requirements to be met and the machines available, in terms of each job which needs to be done. Many standard tools now available are more efficient than high-speed machines if the machines are used as gadgets rather than as the mechanical elements of well-considered systems.

It does not appear impossible for us to learn to think in terms of scientific management to such an extent that we may eventually be able to do much of the routine part of bibliographic work mechanically with greater efficiency, both in terms of cost per unit of service and in terms of management of the intellectual content of literature. There are many bibliographic tasks which will probably not be done mechanically in the near future because the present tools appear to present great advantages over any machine in sight; for example, author bibliography done on the electronic machines would appear to require almost as much work in instructing the machine as is required to look in an author catalog. The major field of usefulness of the machines would appear to be that of subject bibliography, and particularly in research rather than quick reference jobs.

Machines now available or in sight cannot answer a quick reference question either as fast or as economically as will consultation of standard reference works such as dictionaries, encyclopedias, or almanacs, nor would it appear worthwhile to instruct a machine and run the machine to pick out one recent book or "any recent book" in a broad subject field. It would appear, therefore, that high-speed electronic or electrical machinery may be used for bibliographic purposes only in research institutions, at least for the next five or ten years, and their use will probably be limited to research problems in those institutions. It seems quite probable that during the next decade electronic machines, including the Rapid Selector, which was designed with bibliographic purposes in mind, will find application in administrative, office, and business uses to a much greater extent than they will in bibliographic operations.

The shortcomings of machines used as gadgets have been stressed in this paper. Nevertheless, the use of machines for bibliographic purposes is developing, and it is developing rapidly. It appears quite certain that several of the machines and mechanical devices can now perform certain of the routine operations involved in bibliographic work more accurately and more efficiently than these operations can be performed without them.

At least one machine, the Rapid Selector, appears potentially capable of performing higher orders of bibliographic work than we have been able to perform in the past, if and when we learn: (a) what is really needed for the advancement of learning in the way of bibliographic services; and (b) how to utilize the machine efficiently.

There is no magic in machines as such. There will be time-lag in their application, just as there was with the typewriter. The speed and efficiency in handling the mechanical part of bibliographic work, which will determine the point of diminishing returns, depend in large measure on how long it will be before we approach these problems from the point of view of scientific management.

This report cannot solve the problem of bibliographic organization. Machines alone cannot solve the problem. We need to develop systems of handling the mass of bibliographic material, but such systems cannot be developed until we discover and establish our objectives, our plans, our standards, our methods and controls, within the framework of each situation. This may take twenty years or it may take one hundred, but it will come. The termination of how long the time-lag will be rests upon our time-lag in gathering objective information upon which scientific management of literature can be based.

1. On the basis of the above passage, machines will *probably* be MOST useful in
   A. determining the cost per unit of service
   B. quick reference jobs
   C. subject bibliography
   D. title cataloging

2. On the basis of the above passage, the Rapid Selector will *probably* be LEAST used during the next ten years in
   A. administration   B. bibliographic work
   C. business   D. office work

3. It may be inferred from the above passage that is is NOT practical to use machines to do author bibliography because
   A. experienced machine operators are not available
   B. more than one machine is needed for such a task
   C. the results obtained from a machine are unreliable
   D. too much work is involved in instructing the machine

4. On the basis of the above passage, one of the criteria of efficiency is the
   A. amount of work required   B. cost per unit of service
   C. net cost of service   D. number of machines available

5. On the basis of the above passage, the LEAST efficient of the following for quick reference jobs are
   A. bibliographies   B. dictionaries
   C. encyclopedias   D. machines

6. On the basis of the above passage, in the next few years,   6.___
    high-speed electronic machinery will probably be used
    for bibliographic purposes only by
       A. civil engineers
       B. institutions of higher education
       C. publishers
       D. research institutions

7. On the basis of the above passage, the Rapid Selector was   7.___
    designed for use in handling
       A. bibliographic operations
       B. computing problems
       C. photographic reproduction
       D. standard reference works

8. On the basis of the above passage, progress on the   8.___
    development of machines to do bibliographic tasks has
    reached the point at which
       A. all present tools have become obsolete
       B. certain jobs are better performed with machines than
          without them
       C. machines are as efficient in doing quick reference
          jobs as in doing special research jobs
       D. machines are no longer regarded as being too expensive

9. The one of the following which is NOT stated by the above   9.___
    passage to be essential in developing ways of handling
    bibliographic material is
       A. discovering methods and controls
       B. establishing objectives
       C. establishing standards
       D. obtaining historical data

10. The above passage indicates that machines alone will NOT   10.___
    be able to solve the problem of
       A. bibliographic organization
       B. reference work
       C. scientific management
       D. system analysis

11. On the basis of the above passage, the viewpoint of   11.___
    scientific management is essential in
       A. developing the mechanical handling of bibliographic
          work
       B. operating the Rapid Selector
       C. repairing electronic machines
       D. showing that people are always superior to machines
          in bibliographic work

12. On the basis of the above passage, there are machines in   12.___
    existence which
       A. are particularly useful for statistical analysis in
          library work
       B. are the result of scientific management of bibliographic
          work
       C. have not been efficiently utilized for bibliographic
          work
       D. may be installed in a medium-sized library

13. On the basis of the above passage, the scientific manage-   13.____
    ment of literature awaits the
    A. assembling of objective information
    B. compilation of new reference books
    C. development of more complex machines
    D. development of simplified machinery

14. Based on the above passage, it may be INFERRED that the   14.____
    author's attitude toward the use of machines in biblio-
    graphic work is that they
    A. have limited usefulness at the present time
    B. will become useful only if scientific management
       is applied
    C. will probably always be restricted to routine
       operations
    D. will probably never be useful

15. The author of the above passage believes that high-speed   15.____
    machines are BEST adapted to bibliographic work when they
    are used
    A. as gadgets
    B. in place of standard reference works
    C. to perform complex operations
    D. to perform routine operations

Questions 16-25.

DIRECTIONS: Questions 16 through 25 deal with the classification of
              non-fiction books according to the Dewey Classification
              as outlined below. For each book listed, print in the
              space on the right the letter in front of the class to
              which it belongs.

                                    Classification

16. Ernst. WORDS: ENGLISH   A. 000 General Works   16.____
    ROOTS AND HOW THEY GROW
                                   B. 100 Philosophy
17. Faulkner. FROM VERSAILLES   17.____
    TO THE NEW DEAL   C. 200 Religion

18. Fry. CHINESE ART   D. 300 Social Science   18.____

19. Kant. CRITIQUE OF PURE   E. 400 Philology   19.____
    REASON
                                   F. 500 Pure Science
20. Millikan. THE ELECTRON   20.____
                                   G. 600 Applied Science,
21. Morgan. THEORY OF THE GENE   Useful Arts   21.____

22. Raine. THE YEAR ONE; POEMS   H. 700 Fine Arts   22.____

23. Richards. PRINCIPLES OF   I. 800 Literature,   23.____
    LITERARY CRITICISM   Belleslettres

24. Steinberg. BASIC JUDAISM   J. 900 History, Biography   24.____

25. Strachey. QUEEN VICTORIA   25.____

KEY (CORRECT ANSWERS)

1. C		11. A	
2. B		12. C	
3. D		13. A	
4. B		14. A	
5. D		15. D	
6. D		16. E	
7. A		17. J	
8. B		18. H	
9. D		19. B	
10. A		20. F	

21. F
22. I
23. I
24. C
25. J

_____

EXAMINATION SECTION
TEST 1

DIRECTIONS: Each question or incomplete statement is followed by
several suggested answers or completions. Select the
one that BEST answers the question or completes the
statement. *PRINT THE LETTER OF THE CORRECT ANSWER IN
THE SPACE AT THE RIGHT.*

1. A push-button telephone with six buttons, one of which is   1.___
   a *hold* button, is often used when more than one outside
   line is needed.
   If you are talking on one line of this type of telephone
   when another call comes in, what is the procedure to
   follow if you want to answer the second call but keep
   the first call on the line?
   Push the
   A. *hold* button at the same time as you push the *pickup*
      button of the ringing line
   B. *hold* button and then push the *pickup* button of the
      ringing line
   C. *pickup* button of the ringing line and then push
      the *hold* button
   D. *pickup* button of the ringing line and push the
      hold button when you return to the original line

2. Suppose that you are asked to prepare a petty cash state-   2.___
   ment for March. The original and one copy are to go to
   the personnel office. One copy is to go to the fiscal
   office, and another copy is to go to your supervisor.
   The last copy is for your files.
   In preparing the statement and the copies, how many
   sheets of copy paper should you use?
   A. 4   B. 5   C. 6   D. 7

3. Which one of the following is the LEAST important advan-   3.___
   tage of putting the subject of a letter in the heading
   to the right of the address?
   It
   A. makes filing of the copy easier
   B. makes more space available in the body of the letter
   C. simplifies distribution of letters
   D. simplifies determination of the subject of the
      letter

4. Of the following, the MOST efficient way to put 100   4.___
   copies of a one-page letter into 9½" x 4 1/8" envelopes
   for mailing is to fold _____ into an envelope.
   A. each letter and insert it immediately after folding
   B. each letter separately until all 100 are folded;
      then insert each one
   C. the 100 letters two at a time, then separate them
      and insert each one
   D. two letters together, slip them apart, and insert
      each one

5. If you find it necessary to make 150 copies of a single-   5.___
   page memorandum, the MOST important reason for choosing
   to duplicate by stencil rather than by the Xerox
   process is that
       A. the stencil master may be saved and reused
       B. it is a less costly process
       C. it results in a neater-looking product
       D. fewer employees are needed to do the work

6. Of the following, the BEST reason for a clerical unit   6.___
   to have its own duplicating machine is that the unit
       A. uses many forms which it must reproduce internally
       B. must make two copies of each piece of incoming mail
          for a special file
       C. must make seven copies of each piece of outgoing
          mail
       D. must type 200 envelopes each month for distribution
          to the same offices

7. Several offices use the same photocopying machine.   7.___
   If each office must pay its share of the cost of running
   this machine, the BEST way of determining how much of
   this cost should be charged to each of these offices is to
       A. determine the monthly number of photocopies made by
          each office
       B. determine the monthly number of originals submitted
          for photocopying by each office
       C. determine the number of times per day each office
          uses the photocopy machine
       D. divide the total cost of running the photocopy
          machine by the total number of offices using the
          machine

8. Which one of the following would it be BEST to use to   8.___
   indicate that a file folder has been removed from the
   files for temporary use in another office?
   A(n)
       A. cross-reference card   B. tickler file marker
       C. aperture card   D. out guide

9. Which one of the following is the MOST important objec-   9.___
   tive of filing?
       A. Giving a secretary something to do in her spare time
       B. Making it possible to locate information quickly
       C. Providing a place to store unneeded documents
       D. Keeping extra papers from accumulating on workers'
          desks

10. If a check has been made out for an incorrect amount,   10.___
    the BEST action for the writer of the check to take is to
        A. erase the original amount and enter the correct
           amount
        B. cross out the original amount with a single line
           and enter the correct amount above it

     C. black out the original amount so that it cannot be
       read and enter the correct amount above it
     D. write a new check

11. Which one of the following BEST describes the usual   11.___
    arrangement of a tickler file?
     A. Alphabetical   B. Chronological
     C. Numerical   D. Geographical

12. Which one of the following is the LEAST desirable filing   12.___
    practice?
     A. Using staples to keep papers together
     B. Filing all material without regard to date
     C. Keeping a record of all materials removed from the
       files
     D. Writing filing instructions on each paper prior to
       filing

13. Assume that one of your duties is to keep records of the   13.___
    office supplies used by your unit for the purpose of
    ordering new supplies when the old supplies run out.
    The information that will be of MOST help in letting you
    know when to reorder supplies is the
     A. quantity issued   B. quantity received
     C. quantity on hand   D. stock number

Questions 14-19.

DIRECTIONS: Questions 14 through 19 consist of sets of names and
              addresses. In each question, the name and address in
              Column II should be an exact copy of the name and
              address in Column I. If there is:
                a mistake *only* in the name, mark your answer A;
                a mistake *only* in the address, mark your answer B;
                a mistake in *both* name and address, mark your answer C;
                no mistake in *either* name or address, mark your
                answer D.

SAMPLE QUESTION

Column I	Column II
Michael Filbert	Michael Filbert
456 Reade Street	645 Reade Street
New York, N.Y. 10013	New York, N.Y. 10013

Since there is a mistake only in the address (the
street number should be 456 instead of 645), the
answer to the sample question is B.

COLUMN I	COLUMN II	
14. Esta Wong	Esta Wang	14.___
141 West 68 St.	141 West 68 St.	
New York, N.Y. 10023	New York, N.Y. 10023	

COLUMN I	COLUMN II	
15. Dr. Alberto Grosso 3475 12th Avenue Brooklyn, N.Y. 11218	Dr. Alberto Grosso 3475 12th Avenue Brooklyn, N.Y. 11218	15.___
16. Mrs. Ruth Bortlas 482 Theresa Ct. Far Rockaway, N.Y. 11691	Ms. Ruth Bortlas 482 Theresa Ct. Far Rockaway, N.Y. 11169	16.___
17. Mr. and Mrs. Howard Fox 2301 Sedgwick Ave. Bronx, N.Y. 10468	Mr. and Mrs. Howard Fox 231 Sedgwick Ave. Bronx, N.Y. 10468	17.___
18. Miss Marjorie Black 223 East 23 Street New York, N.Y. 10010	Miss Margorie Black 223 East 23 Street New York, N.Y. 10010	18.___
19. Michelle Herman 806 Valley Rd. Old Tappan, N.J. 07675	Michelle Hermann 806 Valley Dr. Old Tappan, N.J. 07675	19.___

Questions 20-25.

DIRECTIONS: Questions 20 through 25 are to be answered SOLELY on the basis of the information in the following passage.

Basic to every office is the need for proper lighting. Inadequate lighting is a familiar cause of fatigue and serves to create a somewhat dismal atmosphere in the office. One requirement of proper lighting is that it be of an appropriate intensity. Intensity is measured in foot-candles. According to the Illuminating Engineering Society of New York, for casual seeing tasks such as in reception rooms, inactive file rooms, and other service areas, it is recommended that the amount of light be 30 foot-candles. For ordinary seeing tasks such as reading and work in active file rooms and in mail rooms, the recommended lighting is 100 foot-candles. For very difficult seeing tasks such as accounting, transcribing, and business machine use, the recommended lighting is 150 foot-candles.

Lighting intensity is only one requirement. Shadows and glare are to be avoided. For example, the larger the proportion of a ceiling filled with lighting units, the more glare-free and comfortable the lighting will be. Natural lighting from windows is not too dependable because on dark wintry days, windows yield little usable light, and on sunny, summer afternoons, the glare from windows may be very distracting. Desks should not face the windows. Finally, the main lighting source ought to be overhead and to the left of the user.

20. According to the above passage, insufficient light in the 20.___
    office may cause
    A. glare   B. shadows
    C. tiredness   D. distraction

21. Based on the above passage, which of the following must   21.___
be considered when planning lighting arrangements?
The
A. amount of natural light present
B. amount of work to be done
C. level of difficulty of work to be done
D. type of activity to be carried out

22. It can be inferred from the above passage that a well-   22.___
coordinated lighting scheme is LIKELY to result in
A. greater employee productivity
B. elimination of light reflection
C. lower lighting cost
D. more use of natural light

23. Of the following, the BEST title for the above passage   23.___
is
A. Characteristics of Light
B. Light Measurement Devices
C. Factors to Consider When Planning Lighting Systems
D. Comfort vs. Cost When Devising Lighting Arrangements

24. According to the above passage, a foot-candle is a   24.___
measurement of the
A. number of bulbs used
B. strength of the light
C. contrast between glare and shadow
D. proportion of the ceiling filled with lighting units

25. According to the above passage, the number of foot-   25.___
candles of light that would be needed to copy figures
onto a payroll is _____ foot-candles.
A. less than 30   B. 30
C. 100   D. 150

KEY (CORRECT ANSWERS)

1. B		11. B	
2. B		12. B	
3. B		13. C	
4. A		14. A	
5. B		15. D	
6. A		16. C	
7. A		17. B	
8. D		18. A	
9. B		19. C	
10. D		20. C	

21. D
22. A
23. C
24. B
25. D

TEST 2

DIRECTIONS: Each question or incomplete statement is followed by several suggested answers or completions. Select the one that BEST answers the question or completes the statement. *PRINT THE LETTER OF THE CORRECT ANSWER IN THE SPACE AT THE RIGHT.*

1. Assume that a supervisor has three subordinates who perform clerical tasks. One of the employees retires and is replaced by someone who is transferred from another unit in the agency. The transferred employee tells the supervisor that she has worked as a clerical employee for two years and understands clerical operations quite well. The supervisor then assigns the transferred employee to a desk, tells the employee to begin working, and returns to his own desk.
   The supervisor's action in this situation is
   A. *proper*; experienced clerical employees do not require training when they are transferred to new assignments
   B. *improper*; before the supervisor returns to his desk, he should tell the other two subordinates to watch the transferred employee perform the work
   C. *proper*; if the transferred employee makes any mistakes, she will bring them to the supervisor's attention
   D. *improper*; the supervisor should find out what clerical tasks the transferred employee has performed and give her instruction in those which are new or different

   1.____

2. Assume that you are falling behind in completing your work assignments and you believe that your workload is too heavy.
   Of the following, the BEST course of action for you to take FIRST is to
   A. discuss the problem with your supervisor
   B. decide which of your assignments can be postponed
   C. try to get some of your co-workers to help you out
   D. plan to take some of the work home with you in order to catch up

   2.____

3. Suppose that one of the clerks under your supervision is filling in monthly personnel forms. She asks you to explain a particular personnel regulation which is related to various items on the forms. You are not thoroughly familiar with the regulation.
   Of the following responses you may make, the one which will gain the MOST respect from the clerk and which is generally the MOST advisable is to
   A. tell the clerk to do the best she can and that you will check her work later
   B. inform the clerk that you are not sure of a correct explanation but suggest a procedure for her to follow

   3.____

      C. give the clerk a suitable interpretation so that she
         will think you are familiar with all regulations
      D. tell the clerk that you will have to read the regula-
         tion more thoroughly before you can give her an
         explanation

4. Charging out records until a specified due date, with   4.___
   prompt follow-up if they are not returned, is a
      A. *good* idea; it may prevent the records from being
         kept needlessly on someone's desk for long periods
         of time
      B. *good* idea; it will indicate the extent of your
         authority to other departments
      C. *poor* idea; the person borrowing the material may
         make an error because of the pressure put upon him
         to return the records
      D. *poor* idea; other departments will feel that you do
         not trust them with the records and they will be
         resentful

Questions 5-9.

DIRECTIONS: Questions 5 through 9 consist of three lines of code
              letters and numbers. The numbers on each line should
              correspond with the code letters on the same line in
              accordance with the table below.

Code Letter	P	L	I	J	B	O	H	U	C	G
Corresponding Number	0	1	2	3	4	5	6	7	8	9

    On some of the lines, an error exists in the coding.
    Compare the letters and numbers in each question care-
    fully. If you find an error or errors on
      only *one* of the lines in the question, mark your answer A
      any *two* lines in the question, mark your answer B;
      all *three* lines in the question, mark your answer C;
      none of the lines in the question, mark your answer D.

SAMPLE QUESTION

JHOILCP   3652180
BICLGUP   4286970
UCIBHLJ   5824613

In the above sample, the first line is correct since each
code letter listed has the correct corresponding number.
On the second line, an error exists because code letter L
should have the number 1 instead of the number 6. On the
third line, an error exists because the code letter U
should have the number 7 instead of the number 5. Since
there are errors on two of the three lines, the correct
answer is B.

5.	BULJCIP	4713920		5.___
	HIGPOUL	6290571		
	OCUHJBI	5876342		
6.	CUBLOIJ	8741023		6.___
	LCLGCLB	1818914		
	JPUHIOC	3076158		
7.	OIJGCBPO	52398405		7.___
	UHPBLIOP	76041250		
	CLUIPGPC	81720908		
8.	BPCOUOJI	40875732		8.___
	UOHCIPLB	75682014		
	GLHUUCBJ	92677843		
9.	HOIOHJLH	65256361		9.___
	IOJJHHBP	25536640		
	OJHBJOPI	53642502		

Questions 10-13.

DIRECTIONS: Questions 10 through 13 are to be answered SOLELY on the basis of the information given in the following passage.

The mental attitude of the employee toward safety is exceedingly important in preventing accidents. All efforts designed to keep safety on the employee's mind and to keep accident prevention a live subject in the office will help substantially in a safety program. Although it may seem strange, it is common for people to be careless. Therefore, safety education is a continuous process.

Safety rules should be explained, and the reasons for their rigid enforcement should be given to employees. Telling employees to be careful or giving similar general safety warnings and slogans is probably of little value. Employees should be informed of basic safety fundamentals. This can be done through staff meetings, informal suggestions to employees, movies, and safety instruction cards. Safety instruction cards provide the employees with specific suggestions about safety and serve as a series of timely reminders helping to keep safety on the minds of employees. Pictures, posters, and cartoon sketches on bulletin boards that are located in areas continually used by employees arouse the employees' interest in safety. It is usually good to supplement this type of safety promotion with intensive individual follow-up.

10. The above passage implies that the LEAST effective of the following safety measures is
    A. rigid enforcement of safety rules
    B. getting employees to think in terms of safety
    C. elimination of unsafe conditions in the office
    D. telling employees to stay alert at all times

10.___

11. The reason given by the passage for maintaining ongoing   11.____
    safety education is that
        A. people are often careless
        B. office tasks are often dangerous
        C. the value of safety slogans increases with repetition
        D. safety rules change frequently

12. Which one of the following safety aids is MOST likely to   12.____
    be preferred by the passage?
    A
        A. cartoon of a man tripping over a carton and yelling,
           Keep aisles clear!
        B. poster with a large number one and a caption saying,
           Safety First
        C. photograph of a very neatly arranged office
        D. large sign with the word *THINK* in capital letters

13. Of the following, the BEST title for the above passage is   13.____
        A. Basic Safety Fundamentals
        B. Enforcing Safety Among Careless Employees
        C. Attitudes Toward Safety
        D. Making Employees Aware of Safety

Questions 14-21.

DIRECTIONS: Questions 14 through 21 are to be answered SOLELY on
              the basis of the information and the chart given below.

    The following chart shows expenses in five selected categories
for a one-year period, expressed as percentages of these same expenses
during the previous year. The chart compares two different offices.
In Office T (represented by [   ]), a cost reduction program has
been tested for the past year. The other office, Office Q (represented
by [////]), served as a control, in that no special effort was made
to reduce costs during the past year.

RESULTS OF OFFICE COST REDUCTION PROGRAM

Expenses of Test and Control Groups for 1989
Expressed as Percentages of Same Expenses for 1988

Test Group (Office T)   Control Group (Office Q)

14. In Office T, which category of expense showed the greatest percentage REDUCTION from 1988 to 1989?   14.___
    A. Telephone   B. Office Supplies
    C. Postage & Mailing   D. Overtime

15. In which expense category did Office T show the BEST results in percentage terms when compared to Office Q?   15.___
    A. Telephone   B. Office Supplies
    C. Postage & Mailing   D. Overtime

16. According to the above chart, the cost reduction program was LEAST effective for the expense category of   16.___
    A. Office Supplies   B. Postage & Mailing
    C. Equipment Repair   D. Overtime

17. Office T's telephone costs went down during 1989 by approximately how many percentage points?   17.___
    A. 15   B. 20   C. 85   D. 105

18. Which of the following changes occurred in expenses for Office Supplies in Office Q in the year 1989 as compared with the year 1988?   18.___
They
    A. increased by more than 100%
    B. remained the same
    C. decreased by a few percentage points
    D. increased by a few percentage points

19. For which of the following expense categories do the results in Office T and the results in Office Q differ MOST NEARLY by 10 percentage points?   19.___
    A. Telephone   B. Postage & Mailing
    C. Equipment Repair   D. Overtime

20. In which expense category did Office Q's costs show the GREATEST percentage increase in 1989?   20.___
    A. Telephone   B. Office Supplies
    C. Postage & Mailing   D. Equipment Repair

21. In Office T, by approximately what percentage did over-time expense change during the past year?   21.___
It
    A. *increased* by 15%   B. *increased* by 75%
    C. *decreased* by 10%   D. *decreased* by 25%

22. In a particular agency, there were 160 accidents in 1987. Of these accidents, 75% were due to unsafe acts and the rest were due to unsafe conditions. In the following year, a special safety program was established. The number of accidents in 1989 due to unsafe acts was reduced to 35% of what it had been in 1987.   22.___
How many accidents due to unsafe acts were there in 1989?
    A. 20   B. 36   C. 42   D. 56

23. At the end of every month, the petty cash fund of Agency   23.___
A is reimbursed for payments made from the fund during
the month. During the month of February, the amounts
paid from the fund were entered on receipts as follows:
10 bus fares of 35¢ each and one taxi fare of $3.50.
At the end of the month, the money left in the fund was
in the following denominations: 15 one dollar bills,
4 quarters, 10 dimes, and 20 nickels.
If the petty cash fund is reduced by 20% for the following month, how much money will there be available in
the petty cash fund for March?
    A. $11.00   B. $20.00   C. $21.50   D. $25.00

24. The one of the following records which it would be MOST   24.___
advisable to keep in alphabetical order is a
    A. continuous listing of phone messages, including
       time and caller, for your supervisor
    B. listing of individuals currently employed by your
       agency in a particular title
    C. record of purchases paid for by the petty cash fund
    D. dated record of employees who have borrowed material
       from the files in your office

25. Assume that you have been asked to copy by hand a column   25.___
of numbers with two decimal places from one record to
another. Each number consists of three, four, and five
digits.
In order to copy them quickly and accurately, you should
copy
    A. each number exactly, making sure that the column of
       digits farthest to the right is in a straight line
       and all other columns are lined up
    B. the column of digits farthest to the right and then
       copy the next column of digits moving from right to
       left
    C. the column of digits farthest to the left and then
       copy the next column of digits moving from left to
       right
    D. the digits to the right of each decimal point and
       then copy the digits to the left of each decimal
       point

KEY (CORRECT ANSWERS)

1. D	6. C	11. A	16. C	21. D
2. A	7. D	12. A	17. A	22. C
3. D	8. B	13. D	18. D	23. B
4. A	9. C	14. D	19. B	24. B
5. A	10. D	15. A	20. C	25. A

EXAMINATION SECTION

TEST 1

DIRECTIONS: Each question or incomplete statement is followed by several suggested answers or completions. Select the one that BEST answers the question or completes the statement. *PRINT THE LETTER OF THE CORRECT ANSWER IN THE SPACE AT THE RIGHT.*

Questions 1-4.

DIRECTIONS: Answer Questions 1 through 4 SOLELY on the basis of the following passage.

Job analysis combined with performance appraisal is an excellent method of determining training needs of individuals. The steps in this method are to determine the specific duties of the job, to evaluate the adequacy with which the employee performs each of these duties, and finally to determine what significant improvements can be made by training.

The list of duties can be obtained in a number of ways: asking the employee, asking the supervisor, observing the employee, etc. Adequacy of performance can be estimated by the employee, but the supervisor's evaluation must also be obtained. This evaluation will usually be based on observation.

What does the supervisor observe? The employee, while he is working; the employee's work relationships; the ease, speed, and sureness of the employee's actions; the way he applies himself to the job; the accuracy and amount of completed work; its conformity with established procedures and standards; the appearance of the work; the soundness of judgment it shows; and, finally, signs of good or poor communication, understanding, and cooperation among employees.

Such observation is a normal and inseparable part of the every-day job of supervision. Systematically recorded, evaluated, and summarized, it highlights both general and individual training needs.

1. According to the passage, job analysis may be used by the supervisor in   1.___
   A. increasing his own understanding of tasks performed in his unit
   B. increasing efficiency of communication within the organization
   C. assisting personnel experts in the classification of positions
   D. determining in which areas an employee needs more instruction

2. According to the passage, the FIRST step in determining   2.___
   the training needs of employees is to
   A. locate the significant improvements that can be
      made by training
   B. determine the specific duties required in a job
   C. evaluate the employee's performance
   D. motivate the employee to want to improve himself

3. On the basis of the above passage, which of the following   3.___
   is the BEST way for a supervisor to determine the adequacy
   of employee performance?
   A. Check the accuracy and amount of completed work
   B. Ask the training officer
   C. Observe all aspects of the employee's work
   D. Obtain the employee's own estimate

4. Which of the following is NOT mentioned by the passage as   4.___
   a factor to be taken into consideration in judging the
   adequacy of employee performance?
   A. Accuracy of completed work
   B. Appearance of completed work
   C. Cooperation among employees
   D. Attitude of the employee toward his supervisor

5. In indexing names of business firms and other organizations,   5.___
   ONE of the rules to be followed is:
   A. The word *and* is considered an indexing unit
   B. When a firm name includes the full name of a person
      who is not well-known, the person's first name is
      considered as the first indexing unit
   C. Usually the units in a firm name are indexed in the
      order in which they are written
   D. When a firm's name is made up of single letters (such
      as ABC Corp.), the letters taken together are con-
      sidered more than one indexing unit

6. Assume that people often come to your office with com-   6.___
   plaints of errors in your agency's handling of their
   clients. The employees in your office have the job of
   listening to these complaints and investigating them.
   One day, when it is almost closing time, a person comes
   into your office, apparently very angry, and demands that
   you take care of his complaint at once.
   Your IMMEDIATE reaction should be to
   A. suggest that he return the following day
   B. find out his name and the nature of his complaint
   C. tell him to write a letter
   D. call over your superior

7. Assume that part of your job is to notify people concerning   7.___
   whether their applications for a certain program have been
   approved or disapproved. However, you do not actually make
   the decision on approval or disapproval. One day, you
   answer a telephone call from a woman who states that she
   has not yet received any word on her application. She goes
   on to tell you her qualifications for the program. From
   what she has said, you know that persons with such qualifications are usually approved.

Of the following, which one is the BEST thing for you to say to her?
- A. "You probably will be accepted, but wait until you receive a letter before trying to join the program."
- B. "Since you seem well qualified, I am sure that your application will be approved."
- C. "If you can write us a letter emphasizing your qualifications, it may speed up the process."
- D. "You will be notified of the results of your application as soon as a decision has been made."

8. Suppose that one of your duties includes answering specific telephone inquiries. Your superior refers a call to you from an irate person who claims that your agency is inefficient and is wasting taxpayers' money.
Of the following, the BEST way to handle such a call is to
- A. listen briefly and then hang up without answering
- B. note the caller's comments and tell him that you will transmit them to your superiors
- C. connect the caller with the head of your agency
- D. discuss your own opinions with the caller

8.___

9. An employee has been assigned to open her division head's mail and place it on his desk. One day, the employee opens a letter which she then notices is marked *Personal*.
Of the following, the BEST action for her to take is to
- A. write *Personal* on the letter and staple the envelope to the back of the letter
- B. ignore the matter and treat the letter the same way as the others
- C. give it to another division head to hold until her own division head comes into the office
- D. leave the letter in the envelope and write *Sorry - opened by mistake* on the envelope and initial it

9.___

Questions 10-14.

DIRECTIONS: Questions 10 through 14 each consist of a quotation which contains one word that is incorrectly used because it is not in keeping with the meaning that the quotation is evidently intended to convey. Of the words underlined in each quotation, determine which word is incorrectly used. Then select from among the words lettered A, B, C, and D the word which, when substituted for the incorrectly used word, would BEST help to convey the meaning of the quotation. (Do NOT indicate a change for an underlined word unless the underlined word is incorrectly used.)

10. Unless reasonable managerial supervision is <u>exercised</u> over office supplies, it is certain that there will be extravagance, <u>rejected</u> items out of stock, <u>excessive</u> prices paid for certain items, and <u>obsolete material</u> in the stockroom.
- A. overlooked
- B. immoderate
- C. needed
- D. instituted

10.___

4 (#1)

11. Since office supplies are in such common use, an
    attitude of indifference about their handling is not
    unusual. Their importance is often recognized only when
    they are utilized or out of stock, for office employees
    must have proper supplies if maximum productivity is to
    be attained.
    A. plentiful   B. unavailable
    C. reduced   D. expected

12. Anyone effected by paperwork, interested in or engaged in
    office work, or desiring to improve informational
    activities can find materials keyed to his needs.
    A. attentive   B. available   C. affected   D. ambitious

13. Information is homogeneous and must therefore be properly
    classified so that each type may be employed in ways
    appropriate to its own peculiar properties.
    A. apparent   B. heterogeneous
    C. consistent   D. idiosyncratic

14. Intellectual training may seem a formidable phrase, but
    it means nothing more than the deliberate cultivation of
    the ability to think, and there is no dark contrast between
    the intellectual and the practical.
    A. subjective   B. objective
    C. sharp   D. vocational

15. The MOST important reason for having a filing system is
    to
    A. get papers out of the way
    B. have a record of everything that has happened
    C. retain information to justify your actions
    D. enable rapid retrieval of information

16. The system of filing which is used MOST frequently is
    called ____ filing.
    A. alphabetic   B. alphanumeric
    C. geographic   D. numeric

17. One of the clerks under your supervision has been tele-
    phoning frequently to tell you that he was taking the day
    off. Unless there is a real need for it, taking leave
    which is not scheduled is frowned upon because it upsets
    the work schedule.
    Under these circumstances, which of the following reasons
    for taking the day off is MOST acceptable?
    A. "I can't work when my arthritis bothers me."
    B. "I've been pressured with work from my night job and
       needed the extra time to catch up."
    C. "My family just moved to a new house, and I needed the
       time to start the repairs."
    D. "Work here has not been challenging, and I've been
       looking for another job."

18. One of the employees under your supervision, previously   18.___
    a very satisfactory worker, has begun arriving late one
    or two mornings each week. No explanation has been
    offered for this change. You call her to your office for
    a conference. As you are explaining the purpose of the
    conference and your need to understand this sudden lateness
    problem, she becomes angry and states that you have no
    right to question her.
    Of the following, the BEST course of action for you to take
    at this point is to
      A. inform her in your most authoritarian tone that you are
         the supervisor and that you have every right to
         question her
      B. end the conference and advise the employee that you
         will have no further discussion with her until she
         controls her temper
      C. remain calm, try to calm her down, and when she has
         quieted, explain the reasons for your questions and
         the need for answers
      D. hold your temper; when she has calmed down, tell her
         that you will not have a tardy worker in your unit
         and will have her transferred at once

19. Assume that, in the branch of the agency for which you   19.___
    work, you are the only clerical person on the staff with
    a supervisory title and, in addition, that you are the
    office manager. On a particular day when all members of
    the professional staff are away from the building attending
    an important meeting, an urgent call comes through re-
    questing some confidential information ordinarily released
    only by professional staff.
    Of the following, the MOST reasonable action for you to
    take is to
      A. decline to give the information because you are not
         a member of the professional staff
      B. offer to call back after you get permission from the
         agency director at the main office
      C. advise the caller that you will supply the information
         as soon as your chief returns
      D. supply the information requested and inform your
         chief when she returns

20. As a supervisor, you are scheduled to attend an important   20.___
    conference with your superior. However, that day you
    learn that your very capable assistant is ill and unable
    to come to work. Several highly sensitive tasks are
    scheduled for completion on this day.
    Of the following, the BEST way to handle this situation
    is to
      A. tell your supervisor you cannot attend the meeting
         and ask that it be postponed
      B. assign one of your staff to see that the jobs are
         completed and turned in
      C. advise your supervisor of the situation and ask
         what you should do
      D. call the departments for which the work is being
         done and ask for an extension of time

21. When a decision needs to be made which is likely to affect units other than his own, a supervisor should USUALLY
    A. make such a decision quickly and then discuss it with his supervisor
    B. make such a decision only after careful consultation with his subordinates
    C. discuss the problem with his immediate superior before making such a decision
    D. have his subordinates arrive at such a decision in conference with the subordinates in the other units

21.___

22. Assume that, as a supervisor in Division X, you are training Ms. Y, a new employee, to answer the telephone properly.
    You should explain that the BEST way to answer is to pick up the receiver and say:
    A. "What is your name, please?"
    B. "May I help you?"
    C. "Ms. Y speaking."
    D. "Division X, Ms. Y speaking."

22.___

Questions 23-25.

DIRECTIONS: Questions 23 through 25 consist of sentences in which two words are missing. Examine each sentence, and then choose from below it the words which should be inserted in the blank spaces in order to create a coherent and well-written sentence.

23. Human behavior is far ____ variable, and therefore ____ predictable, than that of any other species.
    A. less; as   B. less; not
    C. more; not   D. more; less

23.___

24. The ____ limitation of this method is that the results are based ____ a narrow sample.
    A. chief; with   B. chief; on
    C. only; for   D. only; to

24.___

25. Although there ____ a standard procedure for handling these problems, each case often has ____ own unique features.
    A. are; its   B. are; their
    C. is; its   D. is; their

25.___

KEY (CORRECT ANSWERS)

1. D	6. B	11. B	16. A	21. C
2. B	7. D	12. C	17. A	22. D
3. C	8. B	13. B	18. C	23. D
4. D	9. D	14. C	19. B	24. B
5. C	10. C	15. D	20. C	25. C

TEST 2

DIRECTIONS: Each question or incomplete statement is followed by several suggested answers or completions. Select the one that BEST answers your question or completes the statement. *PRINT THE LETTER OF THE CORRECT ANSWER IN THE SPACE AT THE RIGHT.*

Questions 1-3.

DIRECTIONS: Questions 1 through 3 each consist of a group of four sentences. Read each sentence carefully, and select the one of the four in each group which represents the BEST English usage for business letters and reports.

1. A. The chairman himself, rather than his aides, has reviewed the report.
   B. The chairman himself, rather than his aides, have reviewed the report.
   C. The chairmen, not the aide, has reviewed the report.
   D. The aide, not the chairmen, have reviewed the report.   1._____

2. A. Various proposals were submitted but the decision is not been made.
   B. Various proposals has been submitted but the decision has not been made.
   C. Various proposals were submitted but the decision is not been made.
   D. Various proposals have been submitted but the decision has not been made.   2._____

3. A. Everyone were rewarded for his successful attempt.
   B. They were successful in their attempts and each of them was rewarded.
   C. Each of them are rewarded for their successful attempts.
   D. The reward for their successful attempts were made to each of them.   3._____

4. Which of the following is MOST suited to arrangement in chronological order?
   A. Applications for various types and levels of jobs
   B. Issues of a weekly publication
   C. Weekly time cards for all employees for the week of April 21
   D. Personnel records for all employees   4._____

5. Words that are *synonymous* with a given word ALWAYS
   A. have the same meaning as the given word
   B. have the same pronunciation as the given word
   C. have the opposite meaning of the given word
   D. can be rhymed with the given word   5._____

Questions 6-11.

DIRECTIONS: Answer Questions 6 through 11 on the basis of the
following chart showing numbers of errors made by
four clerks in one work unit for a half-year period.

	Allan	Barry	Cary	David
July	5	4	1	7
Aug.	8	3	9	8
Sept.	7	8	7	5
Oct.	3	6	5	3
Nov.	2	4	4	6
Dec.	5	2	8	4

6. The clerk with the HIGHEST number of errors for the six-   6.____
month period was
    A. Allan   B. Barry   C. Cary   D. David

7. If the number of errors made by Allan in the six months   7.____
shown represented one-eighth of the total errors made by
the unit during the entire year, what was the TOTAL
number of errors made by the unit for the year?
    A. 124   B. 180   C. 240   D. 360

8. The number of errors made by David in November was what   8.____
FRACTION of the total errors made in November?
    A. 1/3   B. 1/6   C. 3/8   D. 3/16

9. The average number of errors made per month per clerk was   9.____
MOST NEARLY
    A. 4   B. 5   C. 6   D. 7

10. Of the total number of errors made during the six-month   10.____
period, the percentage made in August was MOST NEARLY
    A. 2%   B. 4%   C. 23%   D. 44%

11. If the number of errors in the unit were to decrease in   11.____
the next six months by 30%, what would be MOST NEARLY the
total number of errors for the unit for the next six months?
    A. 87   B. 94   C. 120   D. 137

12. The arithmetic mean salary for five employees earning   12.____
$18,500, $18,300, $18,600, $18,400, and $18,500, respec-
tively, is
    A. $18,450   B. $18,460   C. $18,475   D. $18,500

13. Last year, a city department which is responsible for   13.___
purchasing supplies ordered bond paper in equal quantities
from 22 different companies. The price was exactly the
same for each company, and the total cost for the 22
orders was $693,113.
Assuming prices did not change during the year, the cost
of EACH order was MOST NEARLY
    A. $31,490   B. $31,495   C. $31,500   D. $31,505

14. A city agency engaged in repair work uses a small part   14.___
which the city purchases for 14¢ each. Assume that, in
a certain year, the total expenditure of the city for
this part was $700.
How MANY of these parts were purchased that year?
    A. 50   B. 200   C. 2,000   D. 5,000

15. The work unit which you supervise is responsible for   15.___
processing fifteen reports per month.
If your unit has four clerks and the best worker completes
40% of the reports himself, how many reports would each
of the other clerks have to complete if they all do an
equal number?
    A. 1   B. 2   C. 3   D. 4

16. Assume that the work unit in which you work has 24 clerks   16.___
and 18 stenographers.
In order to change the ratio of stenographers to clerks
so that there is one stenographer for every four clerks,
it would be necessary to REDUCE the number of stenographers
by
    A. 3   B. 6   C. 9   D. 12

17. Assume that your office is responsible for opening and   17.___
distributing all the mail of the division. After opening
a letter, one of your subordinates notices that it states
that there should be an enclosure in the envelope. However,
there is no enclosure in the envelope.
Of the following, the BEST instruction that you can give
the clerk is to
    A. call the sender to obtain the enclosure
    B. call the addressee to inform him that the enclosure
       is missing
    C. note the omission in the margin of the letter
    D. forward the letter without taking any action

18. While opening the envelope containing official correspon-   18.___
dence, you accidentally cut the enclosed letter.
Of the following, the BEST action for you to take is to
    A. leave the material as it is
    B. put it together by using transparent mending tape
    C. keep it together by putting it back in the envelope
    D. keep it together by using paper clips

19. Suppose your supervisor is on the telephone in his office   19.___
    and an applicant arrives for a scheduled interview with
    him.
    Of the following, the BEST procedure to follow ordinarily
    is to
    A. informally chat with the applicant in your office
       until your supervisor has finished his phone
       conversation
    B. escort him directly into your supervisor's office
       and have him wait for him there
    C. inform your supervisor of the applicant's arrival
       and try to make the applicant feel comfortable while
       waiting
    D. have him hang up his coat and tell him to go directly
       in to see your supervisor

20. The length of time that files should be kept is GENERALLY   20.___
    A. considered to be seven years
    B. dependent upon how much new material has accumulated
       in the files
    C. directly proportionate to the number of years the
       office has been in operation
    D. dependent upon the type and nature of the material
       in the files

21. Cross-referencing a document when you file it means   21.___
    A. making a copy of the document and putting the copy
       into a related file
    B. indicating on the front of the document the name of
       the person who wrote it, the date it was written,
       and for what purpose
    C. putting a special sheet or card in a related file to
       indicate where the document is filed
    D. indicating on the document where it is to be filed

22. Unnecessary handling and recording of incoming mail could   22.___
    be eliminated by
    A. having the person who opens it initial it
    B. indicating on the piece of mail the names of all the
       individuals who should see it
    C. sending all incoming mail to more than one central
       location
    D. making a photocopy of each piece of incoming mail

23. Of the following, the office tasks which lend themselves   23.___
    MOST readily to planning and study are
    A. repetitive, occur in volume, and extend over a
       period of time
    B. cyclical in nature, have small volume, and extend
       over a short period of time
    C. tasks which occur only once in a great while not
       according to any schedule, and have large volume
    D. special tasks which occur only once, regardless of
       their volume and length of time

24. A good recordkeeping system includes all of the following   24.___
procedures EXCEPT the
A. filing of useless records
B. destruction of certain files
C. transferring of records from one type of file to
another
D. creation of inactive files

25. Assume that, as a supervisor, you are responsible for   25.___
orienting and training new employees in your unit.
Which of the following can MOST properly be omitted from
your discussions with a new employee?
A. The purpose of commonly used office forms
B. Time and leave regulations
C. Procedures for required handling of routine business
calls
D. The reason the last employee was fired

KEY (CORRECT ANSWERS)

1. A   11. A
2. D   12. B
3. B   13. D
4. B   14. D
5. A   15. C

6. C   16. D
7. C   17. C
8. C   18. B
9. B   19. C
10. C   20. D

21. C
22. B
23. A
24. A
25. D

READING COMPREHENSION
UNDERSTANDING AND INTERPRETING WRITTEN MATERIAL
EXAMINATION SECTION

DIRECTIONS: Each question or incomplete statement is followed by several suggested answers or completions. Select the one that BEST answers the question or completes the statement. *PRINT THE LETTER OF THE CORRECT ANSWER IN THE SPACE AT THE RIGHT.*

TEST 1

Questions 1-3.

DIRECTIONS: Questions 1 through 3 are to be answered SOLELY on the basis of the following statement.

The equipment in a mailroom may include a mail metering machine. This machine simultaneously stamps, postmarks, seals, and counts letters as fast as the operator can feed them. It can also print the proper postage directly on a gummed strip to be affixed to bulky items. It is equipped with a meter which is removed from the machine and sent to the postmaster to be set for a given number of stampings of any denomination. The setting of the meter must be paid for in advance. One of the advantages of metered mail is that it by-passes the cancellation operation and thereby facilitates handling by the post office. Mail metering also makes the pilfering of stamps impossible, but does not prevent the passage of personal mail in company envelopes through the meters unless there is established a rigid control or censorship over outgoing mail.

1. According to this statement, the postmaster   1.____
   A. is responsible for training new clerks in the use of mail metering machines
   B. usually recommends that both large and small firms adopt the use of mail metering machines
   C. is responsible for setting the meter to print a fixed number of stampings
   D. examines the mail metering machine to see that they are properly installed in the mailroom

2. According to this statement, the use of mail metering   2.____
   machines
   A. requires the employment of more clerks in a mailroom than does the use of postage stamps
   B. interferes with the handling of large quantities of outgoing mail
   C. does not prevent employees from sending their personal letters at company expense
   D. usually involves smaller expenditures for mailroom equipment than does the use of postage stamps

3. On the basis of this statement, it is MOST accurate to   3.___
state that
   A. mail metering machines are often used for opening
      envelopes
   B. postage stamps are generally used when bulky packages
      are to be mailed
   C. the use of metered mail tends to interfere with rapid
      mail handling by the post office
   D. mail metering machines can seal and count letters at
      the same time

Questions 4-5.

DIRECTIONS: Questions 4 and 5 are to be answered SOLELY on the basis
                of the following statement.

     Forms are printed sheets of paper on which information is to be
entered. While what is printed on the form is most important, the
kind of paper used in making the form is also important. The kind of
paper should be selected with regard to the use to which the form
will be subjected. Printing a form on an unnecessarily expensive
grade of papers is wasteful. On the other hand, using too cheap or
flimsy a form can materially interfere with satisfactory performance
of the work the form is being planned to do. Thus, a form printed
on both sides normally requires a heavier paper than a form printed
only on one side. Forms to be used as permanent records, or which
are expected to have a very long life in files, requires a quality
of paper which will not disintegrate or discolor with age. A form
which will go through a great deal of handling requires a strong
tough paper, while thinness is a necessary qualification where the
making of several carbon copies of a form will be required.

4. According to this statement, the type of paper used for   4.___
making forms
   A. should be chosen in accordance with the use to which
      the form will be put
   B. should be chosen before the type of printing to be
      used has been decided upon
   C. is as important as the information which is printed on
      it
   D. should be strong enough to be used for any purpose

5. According to this statement, forms that are   5.___
   A. printed on both sides are usually economical and
      desirable
   B. to be filed permanently should not deteriorate as time
      goes on
   C. expected to last for a long time should be handled
      carefully
   D. to be filed should not be printed on inexpensive paper

Questions 6-8.

DIRECTIONS: Questions 6 through 8 are to be answered SOLELY on the basis of the following paragraph.

The increase in the number of public documents in the last two centuries closely matches the increase in population in the United States. The great number of public documents has become a serious threat to their usefulness. It is necessary to have programs which will reduce the number of public documents that are kept and which will, at the same time, assure keeping those that have value. Such programs need a great deal of thought to have any success.

6. According to the above paragraph, public documents may be   6.___
   LESS useful if
   A. the files are open to the public
   B. the record room is too small
   C. the copying machine is operated only during normal
      working hours
   D. too many records are being kept

7. According to the above paragraph, the growth of the popula-   7.___
   tion in the United States has matched the growth in the
   quantity of public documents for a period of MOST NEARLY
   _____ years.
       A. 50   B. 100   C. 200   D. 300

8. According to the above paragraph, the increased number of   8.___
   public documents has made it necessary to
   A. find out which public documents are worth keeping
   B. reduce the great number of public documents by
      decreasing government services
   C. eliminate the copying of all original public documents
   D. avoid all new copying devices

Questions 9-10.

DIRECTIONS: Questions 9 and 10 are to be answered SOLELY on the basis of the following paragraph.

The work goals of an agency can best be reached if the employees understand and agree with these goals. One way to gain such understanding and agreement is for management to encourage and seriously consider suggestions from employees in the setting of agency goals.

9. On the basis of the above paragraph, the BEST way to   9.___
   achieve the work goals of an agency is to
   A. make certain that employees work as hard as possible
   B. study the organizational structure of the agency
   C. encourage employees to think seriously about the
      agency's problems
   D. stimulate employee understanding of the work goals

10. On the basis of the above paragraph, understanding and   10.____
    agreement with agency goals can be gained by
      A. allowing the employees to set agency goals
      B. reaching agency goals quickly
      C. legislative review of agency operations
      D. employee participation in setting agency goals

Questions 11-13.

DIRECTIONS: Questions 11 through 13 are to be answered SOLELY on
              the basis of the following paragraph.

     In order to organize records properly, it is necessary to start
from their very beginning and trace each copy of the record to find
out how it is used, how long it is used, and what may finally be done
with it. Although several copies of the record are made, one copy
should be marked as the copy of record. This is the formal legal
copy, held to meet the requirements of the law. The other copies may
be retained for brief periods for reference purposes, but these copies
should not be kept after their usefulness as reference ends. There
is another reason for tracing records through the office and that is
to determine how long it takes the copy of record to reach the central
file. The copy of record must not be kept longer than necessary by
the section of the office which has prepared it, but should be sent
to the central file as soon as possible so that it can be available
to the various sections of the office. The central file can make the
copy of record available to the various sections of the office at an
early date only if it arrives at the central file as quickly as
possible. Just as soon as its immediate or active service period is
ended, the copy of record should be removed from the central file
and put into the inactive file in the office to be stored for whatever length of time may be necessary to meet legal requirements, and
then destroyed.

11. According to the above paragraph, a reason for tracing   11.____
    records through an office is to
      A. determine how long the central file must keep the
         records
      B. organize records properly
      C. find out how many copies of each record are required
      D. identify the copy of record

12. According to the above paragraph, in order for the central   12.____
    file to have the copy of record available as soon as
    possible for the various sections of the office, it is
    MOST important that the
      A. copy of record to be sent to the central file meets
         the requirements of the law
      B. copy of record is not kept in the inactive file too
         long
      C. section preparing the copy of record does not unduly
         delay in sending it to the central file
      D. central file does not keep the copy of record beyond
         its active service period

4

13. According to the above paragraph, the length of time a   13.___
    copy of a record is kept in the inactive file of an office
    depends CHIEFLY on the
    A. requirements of the law
    B. length of time that is required to trace the copy of
       record through the office
    C. use that is made of the copy of record
    D. length of the period that the copy of record is used
       for reference purposes

Questions 14-16.

DIRECTIONS: Questions 14 through 16 are to be answered SOLELY on
              the basis of the following paragraph.

The office was once considered as nothing more than a focal point
of internal and external correspondence. It was capable only of dis-
patching a few letters upon occasion and of preparing records of
little practical value. Under such a concept, the vitality of the
office force was impaired. Initiative became stagnant, and the lot of
the office worker was not likely to be a happy one. However, under
the new concept of office management, the possibilities of waste and
mismanagement in office operation are now fully recognized, as are
the possibilities for the modern office to assist in the direction
and control of business operations. Fortunately, the modern concept
of the office as a centralized service-rendering unit is gaining ever
greater acceptance in today's complex business world, for without
the modern office, the production wheels do not turn and the distribution of goods and services is not possible.

14. According to the above paragraph, the fundamental   14.___
    difference between the old and the new concept of the
    office is the change in the
    A. accepted functions of the office
    B. content and the value of the records kept
    C. office methods and systems
    D. vitality and morale of the office force

15. According to the above paragraph, an office operated   15.___
    today under the old concept of the office MOST likely
    would
    A. make older workers happy in their jobs
    B. be part of an old thriving business concern
    C. have a passive role in the conduct of a business
       enterprise
    D. attract workers who do not believe in modern methods

16. Of the following, the MOST important implication of the   16.___
    above paragraph is that a present day business organization
    cannot function effectively without the
    A. use of modern office equipment
    B. participation and cooperation of the office
    C. continued modernization of office procedures
    D. employment of office workers with skill and initiative

Questions 17-20.

DIRECTIONS: Questions 17 through 20 are to be answered SOLELY on the basis of the following paragraph.

A report is frequently ineffective because the person writing it is not fully acquainted with all the necessary details before he actually starts to construct the report. All details pertaining to the subject should be known before the report is started. If the essential facts are not known, they should be investigated. It is wise to have essential facts written down rather than to depend too much on memory, especially if the facts pertain to such matters as amounts, dates, names of persons, or other specific data. When the necessary information has been gathered, the general plan and content of the report should be thought out before the writing is actually begun. A person with little or no experience in writing reports may find that it is wise to make a brief outline. Persons with more experience should not need a written outline, but they should make mental notes of the steps they are to follow. If writing reports without dictation is a regular part of an office worker's duties, he should set aside a certain time during the day when he is least likely to be interrupted. That may be difficult, but in most offices there are certain times in the day when the callers, telephone calls, and other interruptions are not numerous. During those times, it is best to write reports that need undivided concentration. Reports that are written amid a series of interruptions may be poorly done.

17. Before starting to write an effective report, it is necessary to
    A. memorize all specific information
    B. disregard ambiguous data
    C. know all pertinent information
    D. develop a general plan

17.____

18. Reports dealing with complex and difficult material should be
    A. prepared and written by the supervisor of the unit
    B. written when there is the least chance of interruption
    C. prepared and written as part of regular office routine
    D. outlined and then dictated

18.____

19. According to the paragraph, employees with no prior familiarity in writing reports may find it helpful to
    A. prepare a brief outline
    B. mentally prepare a synopsis of the report's content
    C. have a fellow employee help in writing the report
    D. consult previous reports

19.____

20. In writing a report, needed information which is unclear should be
    A. disregarded   B. investigated
    C. memorized   D. gathered

20.____

Questions 21-25.

DIRECTIONS: Questions 21 through 25 are to be answered SOLELY on the basis of the following passage.

Positive discipline minimizes the amount of personal supervision required and aids in the maintenance of standards. When a new employee has been properly introduced and carefully instructed, when he has come to know the supervisor and has confidence in the supervisor's ability to take care of him, when he willingly cooperates with the supervisor, that employee has been under positive discipline and can be put on his own to produce the quantity and quality of work desired. Negative discipline, the fear of transfer to a less desirable location, for example, to a limited extent may restrain certain individuals from overt violation of rules and regulations governing attendance and conduct which in governmental agencies are usually on at least an agency-wide basis. Negative discipline may prompt employees to perform according to certain rules to avoid a penalty such as, for example, docking for tardiness.

21. According to the above passage, it is reasonable to assume   21.____
    that in the area of discipline, the first-line supervisor
    in a governmental agency has GREATER scope for action in
    A. *positive* discipline, because negative discipline is
        largely taken care of by agency rules and regulations
    B. *negative* discipline, because rules and procedures are
        already fixed and the supervisor can rely on them
    C. *positive* discipline, because the supervisor is in a
        position to recommend transfers
    D. *negative* discipline, because positive discipline is
        reserved for people on a higher supervisory level

22. In order to maintain positive discipline of employees   22.____
    under his supervision, it is MOST important for a super-
    visor to
    A. assure each employee that he has nothing to worry about
    B. insist at the outset on complete cooperation from
        employees
    C. be sure that each employee is well trained in his job
    D. inform new employees of the penalties for not
        meeting standards

23. According to the above passage, a feature of negative   23.____
    discipline is that it
    A. may lower employee morale
    B. may restrain employees from disobeying the rules
    C. censures equal treatment of employees
    D. tends to create standards for quality of work

24. A REASONABLE conclusion based on the above passage is   24.____
    that positive discipline benefits a supervisor because
    A. he can turn over orientation and supervision of a new
        employee to one of his subordinates
    B. subordinates learn to cooperate with one another when
        working on an assignment

   C. it is easier to administer
   D. it cuts down, in the long run, on the amount of time
    the supervisor needs to spend on direct supervision

25. Based on the above passage, it is REASONABLE to assume   25.___
  that an important difference between positive discipline
  and negative discipline is that positive discipline
    A. is concerned with the quality of work and negative
     discipline with the quantity of work
    B. leads to a more desirable basis for motivation of
     the employee
    C. is more likely to be concerned with agency rules and
     regulations
    D. uses fear while negative discipline uses penalties
     to prod employees to adequate performance

TEST 2

Questions 1-6.

DIRECTIONS: Questions 1 through 6 are to be answered SOLELY on the
     basis of the following passage.

  Inherent in all organized endeavors is the need to resolve the
individual differences involved in conflict. Conflict may be either
a positive or negative factor since it may lead to creativity, inno-
vation and progress on the one hand, or it may result, on the other
hand, in a deterioration or even destruction of the organization.
Thus, some forms of conflict are desirable, whereas others are
undesirable and ethically wrong.

  There are three management strategies which deal with interpersonal conflict. In the *divide-and-rule strategy*, management
attempts to maintain control by limiting the conflict to those directly
involved and preventing their disagreement from spreading to the
larger group. The *suppression-of-differences strategy* entails ignor-
ing conflicts or pretending they are irrelevant. In the *working-
through-differences strategy*, management actively attempts to solve
or resolve intergroup or interpersonal conflicts. Of the three
strategies, only the last directly attacks and has the potential for
eliminating the causes of conflict. An essential part of this
strategy, however, is its employment by a committed and relatively
mature management team.

1. According to the above passage, the *divide-and-rule*   1.___
  strategy for dealing with conflict is the attempt to
    A. involve other people in the conflict
    B. restrict the conflict to those participating in it
    C. divide the conflict into positive and negative factors
    D. divide the conflict into a number of smaller ones

2. The word *conflict* is used in relation to both positive and   2.___
    negative factors in this passage.
    Which one of the following words is MOST likely to describe
    the activity which the word *conflict*, in the sense of the
    passage, implies?
    A. Competition   B. Cooperation
    C. Confusion   D. Aggression

3. According to the above passage, which one of the following   3.___
    characteristics is shared by both the *suppression-of-
    differences strategy* and the *divide-and-rule strategy*?
    A. Pretending that conflicts are irrelevant
    B. Preventing conflicts from spreading to the group
       situation
    C. Failure to directly attack the causes of conflict
    D. Actively attempting to resolve interpersonal conflict

4. According to the above passage, the successful resolution   4.___
    of interpersonal conflict requires
    A. allowing the group to mediate conflicts between two
       individuals
    B. division of the conflict into positive and negative
       factors
    C. involvement of a committed, mature management team
    D. ignoring minor conflicts until they threaten the
       organization

5. Which can be MOST reasonably inferred from the above   5.___
    passage?
    A conflict between two individuals is LEAST likely to
    continue when management uses
    A. the *working-through-differences strategy*
    B. the *suppression-of-differences strategy*
    C. the *divide-and-rule strategy*
    D. a combination of all three strategies

6. According to the above passage, a DESIRABLE result of   6.___
    conflict in an organization is when conflict
    A. exposes production problems in the organization
    B. can be easily ignored by management
    C. results in advancement of more efficient managers
    D. leads to development of new methods

Questions 7-13.

DIRECTIONS: Questions 7 through 13 are to be answered SOLELY on
             the basis of the passage below.

    Modern management places great emphasis on the concept of communi-
cation. The communication process consists of the steps through which
an idea or concept passes from its inception by one person, the
sender, until it is acted upon by another person, the receiver. Through
an understanding of these steps and some of the possible barriers that
may occur, more effective communication may be achieved. The first

step in the communication process is ideation by the sender. This is the formation of the intended content of the message he wants to transmit. In the next step, encoding, the sender organizes his ideas into a series of symbols designed to communicate his message to his intended receiver. He selects suitable words or phrases that can be understood by the receiver, and he also selects the appropriate media to be used -- for example, memorandum, conference, etc. The third step is transmission of the encoded message through selected channels in the organizational structure. In the fourth step, the receiver enters the process by tuning in to receive the message. If the receiver does not function, however, the message is lost. For example, if the message is oral, the receiver must be a good listener. The fifth step is decoding of the message by the receiver, as for example, by changing words into ideas. At this step, the decoded message may not be the same idea that the sender originally encoded because the sender and receiver have different perceptions regarding the meaning of certain words. Finally, the receiver acts or responds. He may file the information, ask for more information, or take other action. There can be no assurance, however, that communication has taken place unless there is some type of feedback to the sender in the form of an acknowledgement that the message was received.

7. According to the above passage, *ideation* is the process   7.___
   by which the
   A. sender develops the intended content of the message
   B. sender organizes his ideas into a series of symbols
   C. receiver tunes in to receive the message
   D. receiver decodes the message

8. In the last sentence of the passage, the word *feedback*   8.___
   refers to the process by which the sender is assured that
   the
   A. receiver filed the information
   B. receiver's perception is the same as his own
   C. message was received
   D. message was properly interpreted

9. Which one of the following BEST shows the order of the   9.___
   steps in the communication process as described in the
   passage?
   A. 1 - ideation   2 - encoding
      3 - decoding   4 - transmission
      5 - receiving   6 - action
      7 - feedback to the sender

   B. 1 - ideation   2 - encoding
      3 - transmission   4 - decoding
      5 - receiving   6 - action
      7 - feedback to the sender

   C. 1 - ideation   2 - decoding
      3 - transmission   4 - receiving
      5 - encoding   6 - action
      7 - feedback to the sender

10

        D. 1 - ideation   2 - encoding
           3 - transmission   4 - receiving
           5 - decoding   6 - action
           7 - feedback to the sender

10. Which one of the following BEST expresses the main theme   10.___
    of the passage?
       A. Different individuals have the same perceptions
          regarding the meaning of words.
       B. An understanding of the steps in the communication
          process may achieve better communication.
       C. Receivers play a passive role in the communication
          process.
       D. Senders should not communicate with receivers who
          transmit feedback.

11. The above passage implies that a receiver does NOT   11.___
    function properly when he
       A. transmits feedback   B. files the information
       C. is a poor listener   D. asks for more information

12. Which one of the following, according to the above   12.___
    passage, is included in the SECOND step of the communica-
    tion process?
       A. Selecting the appropriate media to be used in trans-
          mission
       B. Formulation of the intended content of the message
       C. Using appropriate media to respond to the receiver's
          feedback
       D. Transmitting the message through selected channels
          in the organization

13. The above passage implies that the *decoding process* is   13.___
    MOST NEARLY the reverse of the _____ process.
       A. transmission   B. receiving
       C. feedback   D. encoding

Questions 14-19.

DIRECTIONS: Questions 14 through 19 are to be answered SOLELY on
             the basis of the following passage.

    It is often said that no system will work if the people who carry
it out do not want it to work. In too many cases, a departmental
reorganization that seemed technically sound and economically practical has proved to be a failure because the planners neglected to
take the human factor into account. The truth is that employees are
likely to feel threatened when they learn that a major change is in
the wind. It does not matter whether or not the change actually
poses a threat to an employee; the fact that he believes it does or
fears it might is enough to make him feel insecure. Among the dangers he fears, the foremost is the possibility that his job may
cease to exist and that he may be laid off or shunted into a less
skilled position at lower pay. Even if he knows that his own job

11

category is secure, however, he is likely to fear losing some of the important intangible advantages of his present position -- for instance, he may fear that he will be separated from his present companions and thrust in with a group of strangers, or that he will find himself in a lower position on the organizational ladder if a new position is created above his.

It is important that management recognize these natural fears and take them into account in planning any kind of major change. While there is no cut-and-dried formula for preventing employee resistance, there are several steps that can be taken to reduce employees' fears and gain their cooperation. First, unwarranted fears can be dispelled if employees are kept informed of the planning from the start and if they know exactly what to expect. Next, assurance on matters such as retraining, transfers, and placement help should be given as soon as it is clear what direction the reorganization will take. Finally, employees' participation in the planning should be actively sought. There is a great psychological difference between feeling that a change is being forced upon one from the outside, and feeling that one is an insider who is helping to bring about a change.

14. According to the above passage, employees who are not in real danger of losing their jobs because of a proposed reorganization   14.___
    A. will be eager to assist in the reorganization
    B. will pay little attention to the reorganization
    C. should not be taken into account in planning the reorganization
    D. are nonetheless likely to feel threatened by the reorganization

15. The passage mentions the *intangible advantages* of a position.   15.___
Which of the following BEST describes the kind of advantages alluded to in the passage?
    A. Benefits such as paid holidays and vacations
    B. Satisfaction of human needs for things like friendship and status
    C. Qualities such as leadership and responsibility
    D. A work environment that meets satisfactory standards of health and safety

16. According to the passage, an employee's fear that a reorganization may separate him from his present companions is a(n)   16.___
    A. childish and immature reaction to change
    B. unrealistic feeling since this is not going to happen
    C. possible reaction that the planners should be aware of
    D. incentive to employees to participate in the planning

17. On the basis of the above passage, it would be DESIRABLE, when planning a departmental reorganization, to   17.___
    A. be governed by employee feelings and attitudes
    B. give some employees lower positions

C. keep employees informed
D. lay off those who are less skilled

18. What does the passage say can be done to help gain   18.___
    employees' cooperation in a reorganization?
    A. Making sure that the change is technically sound, that
       it is economically practical, and that the human factor
       is taken into account
    B. Keeping employees fully informed, offering help in
       fitting them into new positions, and seeking their
       participation in the planning
    C. Assuring employees that they will not be laid off,
       that they will not be reassigned to a group of strangers,
       and that no new positions will be created on the
       organization ladder
    D. Reducing employees' fears, arranging a retraining
       program, and providing for transfers

19. Which of the following suggested titles would be MOST   19.___
    appropriate for this passage?
    A. PLANNING A DEPARTMENTAL REORGANIZATION
    B. WHY EMPLOYEES ARE AFRAID
    C. LOOKING AHEAD TO THE FUTURE
    D. PLANNING FOR CHANGE: THE HUMAN FACTOR

Questions 20-22.

DIRECTIONS: Questions 20 through 22 are to be answered SOLELY on
             the basis of the following passage.

     The achievement of good human relations is essential if a business
office is to produce at top efficiency and is to be a pleasant place in
which to work. All office workers plan an important role in handling
problems in human relations. They should, therefore, strive to
acquire the understanding, tactfulness, and awareness necessary to
deal effectively with actual office situations involving co-workers
on all levels. Only in this way can they truly become responsible,
interested, cooperative, and helpful members of the staff.

20. The selection implies that the MOST important value of   20.___
    good human relations in an office is to develop
    A. efficiency   B. cooperativeness
    C. tact   D. pleasantness and efficiency

21. Office workers should acquire understanding in dealing   21.___
    with
    A. co-workers   B. subordinates
    C. superiors   D. all members of the staff

22. The selection indicates that a highly competent secretary   22.___
    who is also very argumentative is meeting office require-
    ments
    A. wholly   B. partly
    C. slightly   D. not at all

13

Questions 23-25.

DIRECTIONS: Questions 23 through 25 are to be answered SOLELY on
                         the basis of the following passage.

It is common knowledge that ability to do a particular job and performance on the job do not always go hand in hand. Persons with great potential abilities sometimes fall down on the job because of laziness or lack of interest in the job, while persons with mediocre talents have often achieved excellent results through their industry and their loyalty to the interests of their employers. It is clear, therefore, that in a balanced personnel program, measures of employee ability need to be supplemented by measures of employee performance, for the final test of any employee is his performance on the job.

23.   The MOST accurate of the following statements, on the basis 23.____
        of the above paragraph, is that
        A. employees who lack ability are usually not industrious
        B. an employee's attitudes are more important than his
             abilities
        C. mediocre employees who are interested in their work are
             preferable to employees who possess great ability
        D. superior capacity for performance should be supplemented
             with proper attitudes

24.   On the basis of the above paragraph, the employee of most   24.____
        value to his employer is NOT necessarily the one who
        A. best understands the significance of his duties
        B. achieves excellent results
        C. possesses the greatest talents
        D. produces the greatest amount of work

25.   According to the above paragraph, an employee's efficiency   25.____
        is BEST determined by an
        A. appraisal of his interest in his work
        B. evaluation of the work performed by him
        C. appraisal of his loyalty to his employer
        D. evaluation of his potential ability to perform his work

---

TEST 3

Questions 1-8.

DIRECTIONS: Questions 1 through 8 are to be answered SOLELY on
                         the basis of the following information and directions.

Assume that you are a clerk in a city agency. Your supervisor has asked you to classify each of the accidents that happened to employees in the agency into the following five categories:

A. An accident that occurred in the period from January through June, between 9 A.M. and 12 Noon, that was the result of carelessness on the part of the injured employee, that caused the employee to lose less than seven working hours, that happened to an employee who was 40 years of age or over, and who was employed in the agency for less than three years;

B. An accident that occurred in the period from July through December, after 1 P.M., that was the result of unsafe conditions, that caused the injured employee to lose less than seven working hours, that happened to an employee who was 40 years of age or over, and who was employed in the agency for three years or more;

C. An accident that occurred in the period from January through June, after 1 P.M., that was the result of carelessness on the part of the injured employee, that caused the injured employee to lose seven or more working hours, that happened to an employee who was less than 40 years old, and who was employed in the agency for three years or more;

D. An accident that occurred in the period from July through December, between 9 A.M. and 12 Noon, that was the result of unsafe conditions, that caused the injured employee to lose seven or more working hours, that happened to an employee who was less than 40 years old, and who was employed in the agency for less than three years;

E. Accidents that cannot be classified in any of the foregoing groups.

NOTE: In classifying these accidents, an employee's age and length of service are computed as of the date of accident. In all cases, it is to be assumed that each employee has been employed continuously in city service, and that each employee works seven hours a day, from 9 A.M. to 5 P.M., with lunch from 12 Noon to 1 P.M. In each question, consider only the information which will assist you in classifying the accident. Any information which is of no assistance in classifying an accident should not be considered.

1. The unsafe condition of the stairs in the building caused   1.___
    Miss Perkins to have an accident on October 14, 1978 at
    4 P.M. When she returned to work the following day at
    1 P.M., Miss Perkins said that the accident was the first
    one that had occurred to her in her ten years of employment
    with the agency. She was born on April 27, 1937.

2. On the day after she completed her six-month probationary   2.___
    period of employment with the agency, Miss Green, who had
    been considered a careful worker by her supervisor, injured
    her left foot in an accident caused by her own carelessness.
    She went home immediately after the accident, which occurred
    at 10 A.M., March 19, 1979, but returned to work at the
    regular time on the following morning. Miss Green was born
    July 12, 1938 in New York City.

15

3. The unsafe condition of a mimeograph machine caused Mr.   3.___
   Martin to injure himself in an accident on September 8,
   1981 at 2 P.M. As a result of the accident, he was unable
   to work the remainder of the day, but returned to his
   office ready for work on the following morning. Mr. Martin,
   who has been working for the agency since April 1, 1978,
   was born in St. Louis on February 1, 1943.

4. Mr. Smith was hospitalized for two weeks because of a back 4.___
   injury which resulted from an accident on the morning of
   November 16, 1981. Investigation of the accident revealed
   that it was caused by the unsafe condition of the floor on
   which Mr. Smith had been walking. Mr. Smith, who is an
   accountant, has been an employee of the agency since March 1,
   1979, and was born in Ohio on June 10, 1943.

5. Mr. Allen cut his right hand because he was careless in   5.___
   operating a multilith machine. Mr. Allen, who was 33 years
   old when the accident took place, has been employed by the
   agency since August 17, 1977. The accident, which occurred
   on January 26, 1981, at 2 P.M., caused Mr. Allen to be
   absent from work for the rest of the day. He was able to
   return to work the next morning.

6. Mr. Rand, who is a college graduate, was born on December   6.___
   28, 1942, and has been working for the agency since
   January 7, 1977. On Monday, April 25, 1980, at 2 P.M.,
   his carelessness in operating a duplicating machine caused
   him to have an accident and to be sent home from work
   immediately. Fortunately, he was able to return to work
   at his regular time on the following Wednesday.

7. Because he was careless in running down a flight of stairs, 7.___
   Mr. Brown fell, bruising his right hand. Although the
   accident occurred shortly after he arrived for work on the
   morning of May 22, 1981, he was unable to resume work until
   3 P.M. that day. Mr. Brown was born on August 15, 1930, and
   began working for the agency on September 12, 1978, as a
   clerk, at a salary of $12,750 per annum.

8. On December 5, 1980, four weeks after he had begun working 8.___
   for the agency, the unsafe condition of an automatic
   stapling machine caused Mr. Thomas to injure himself in an
   accident. Mr. Thomas, who was born on May 19, 1950, lost
   three working days because of the accident, which occurred
   at 11:45 A.M.

Questions 9-10.

DIRECTIONS: Questions 9 and 10 are to be answered SOLELY on the basis of the following paragraph.

An impending reorganization within an agency will mean loss by transfer of several professional staff members from the personnel division. The division chief is asked to designate the persons to be transferred. After reviewing the implications of this reduction of staff with his assistant, the division chief discusses the matter at a staff meeting. He adopts the recommendations of several staff members to have volunteers make up the required reduction.

9. The decision to permit personnel to volunteer for transfer is   9.___
   A. *poor*; it is not likely that the members of a division are of equal value to the division chief
   B. *good*; dissatisfied members will probably be more productive elsewhere
   C. *poor*; the division chief has abdicated his responsibility to carry out the order given to him
   D. *good*; morale among remaining staff is likely to improve in a more cohesive framework

10. Suppose that one of the volunteers is a recently appointed   10.___
    employee who has completed his probationary period acceptably, but whose attitude toward division operations and agency administration tends to be rather negative and sometimes even abrasive. Because of his lack of commitment to the division, his transfer is recommended.
    If the transfer is approved, the division chief should, prior to the transfer,
    A. discuss with the staff the importance of commitment to the work of the agency and its relationship with job satisfaction
    B. refrain from any discussion of attitude with the employee
    C. discuss with the employee his concern about the employee's attitude
    D. avoid mention of attitude in the evaluation appraisal prepared for the receiving division chief

Questions 11-16.

DIRECTIONS: Questions 11 through 16 are to be answered SOLELY on the basis of the following paragraph.

Methods of administration of office activities, much of which consists of providing information and *know-how* needed to coordinate both activities within that particular office and other offices, have been among the last to come under the spotlight of management analysis. Progress has been rapid during the past decade, however, and is now accelerating at such a pace that an *information revolution* in office management appears to be in the making. Although triggered by technological breakthroughs in electronic computers and other giant steps in mechanization, this information revolution must be attributed to underlying forces, such as the increased complexity of both governmental and private enterprise, and ever-keener competition. Size, diversification, specialization of function, and decentralization are among the forces which make coordination of activities both more imperative and more difficult. Increased competition, both domestic and international, leaves little margin for error in managerial decisions. Several developments during recent years indicate an evolving pattern. In 1960, the American Management Association expanded the scope of its activities and changed the name of its Office Management Division to Administrative Services Division. Also in 1960, the magazine *Office Management* merged with the magazine *American Business*, and this new publication was named *Administrative Management*.

11. A REASONABLE inference that can be made from the information in the above paragraph is that an important role of the office manager today is to   11.___
    - A. work toward specialization of functions performed by his subordinates
    - B. inform and train subordinates regarding any new developments in computer technology and mechanization
    - C. assist the professional management analysts with the management analysis work in the organization
    - D. supply information that can be used to help coordinate and manage the other activities of the organization

12. An IMPORTANT reason for the *information revolution* that has been taking place in office management is the   12.___
    - A. advance made in management analysis in the past decade
    - B. technological breakthrough in electronic computers and mechanization
    - C. more competitive and complicated nature of private business and government
    - D. increased efficiency of office management techniques in the past ten years

13. According to the above paragraph, specialization of function in an organization is MOST likely to result in   13.___
    - A. the elimination of errors in managerial decisions
    - B. greater need to coordinate activities
    - C. more competition with other organizations, both domestic and international
    - D. a need for office managers with greater flexibility

14. The word *evolving*, as used in the third from last sentence in the above paragraph, means MOST NEARLY   14.___
    - A. developing by gradual changes
    - B. passing on to others
    - C. occurring periodically
    - D. breaking up into separate, constituent parts

15. Of the following, the MOST reasonable implication of the   15.___
    changes in names mentioned in the last part of the above
    paragraph is that these groups are attempting to
    A. professionalize the field of office management and
       the title of Office Manager
    B. combine two publications into one because of the
       increased costs of labor and materials
    C. adjust to the fact that the field of office manage-
       ment is broadening
    D. appeal to the top managerial people rather than the
       office management people in business and government

16. According to the above paragraph, intense competition   16.___
    among domestic and international enterprises makes it
    MOST important for an organization's managerial staff to
    A. coordinate and administer office activities with other
       activities in the organization
    B. make as few errors in decision-making as possible
    C. concentrate on decentralization and reduction of size
       of the individual divisions of the organization
    D. restrict decision-making only to top management
       officials

Questions 17-21.

DIRECTIONS: Questions 17 through 21 are to be answered SOLELY on
              the basis of the following passage.

For some office workers, it is useful to be familiar with the
four main classes of domestic mail; for others, it is essential. Each
class has a different rate of postage, and some have requirements
concerning wrapping, sealing, or special information to be placed on
the package. First class mail, the class which may not be opened for
postal inspection, includes letters, postcards, business reply cards,
and other kinds of written matter. There are different rates for
some of the kinds of cards which can be sent by first class mail. The
maximum weight for an item sent by first class mail is 70 pounds. An
item which is not letter size should be marked *First Class* on all
sides.

Although office workers most often come into contact with first
class mail, they may find it helpful to know something about the
other classes. Second class mail is generally used for mailing
newspapers and magazines. Publishers of these articles must meet
certain U.S. Postal Service requirements in order to obtain a permit
to use second class mailing rates. Third class mail, which must
weigh less than 1 pound, includes printed materials and merchandise
parcels. There are two rate structures for this class - a single
piece rate and a bulk rate. Fourth class mail, also known as parcel
post, includes packages weighing from one to 40 pounds. For more
information about these classes of mail and the actual mailing rates,
contact your local post office.

17. According to this passage, first class mail is the *only*   17.___
      class which
        A. has a limit on the maximum weight of an item
        B. has different rates for items within the class
        C. may not be opened for postal inspection
        D. should be used by office workers

18. According to this passage, the one of the following items   18.___
      which may CORRECTLY be sent by fourth class mail is a
        A. magazine weighing one-half pound
        B. package weighing one-half pound
        C. package weighing two pounds
        D. postcard

19. According to this passage, there are different postage   19.___
      rates for
        A. a newspaper sent by second class mail and a magazine
           sent by second class mail
        B. each of the classes of mail
        C. each pound of fourth class mail
        D. printed material sent by third class mail and
           merchandise parcels sent by third class mail

20. In order to send a newspaper by second class mail, a   20.___
      publisher MUST
        A. have met certain postal requirements and obtained a
           permit
        B. indicate whether he wants to use the single piece
           or the bulk rate
        C. make certain that the newspaper weighs less than one
           pound
        D. mark the newspaper *Second Class* on the top and bottom
           of the wrapper

21. Of the following types of information, the one which is   21.___
      NOT mentioned in the passage is the
        A. class of mail to which parcel post belongs
        B. kinds of items which can be sent by each class of mail
        C. maximum weight for an item sent by fourth class mail
        D. postage rate for each of the four classes of mail

Questions 22-25.

DIRECTIONS: Questions 22 through 25 are to be answered SOLELY on
                the basis of the following paragraph.

    A standard comprises characteristics attached to an aspect of a
process or product by which it can be evaluated. Standardization is
the development and adoption of standards. When they are formulated,
standards are not usually the product of a single person, but represent the thoughts and ideas of a group, leavened with the knowledge
and information which are currently available. Standards which do
not meet certain basic requirements become a hindrance rather than an
aid to progress. Standards must not only be correct, accurate, and

precise in requiring no more and no less than what is needed for satisfactory results, but they must also be workable in the sense that their usefulness is not nullified by external conditions. Standards should also be acceptable to the people who use them. If they are not acceptable, they cannot be considered to be satisfactory, although they may possess all the other essential characteristics.

22. According to the above paragraph, a processing standard   22.____
     that requires the use of materials that cannot be procured
     is MOST likely to be
         A. incomplete   B. inaccurate
         C. unworkable   D. unacceptable

23. According to the above paragraph, the construction of   23.____
     standards to which the performance of job duties should
     conform is MOST often
         A. the work of the people responsible for seeing that the
            duties are properly performed
         B. accomplished by the person who is best informed about
            the functions involved
         C. the responsibility of the people who are to apply them
         D. attributable to the efforts of various informed persons

24. According to the above paragraph, when standards call for   24.____
     finer tolerances than those essential to the conduct of
     successful production operations, the effect of the
     standards on the improvement of production operations is
         A. negative   B. nullified
         C. negligible   D. beneficial

25. The one of the following which is the MOST suitable title   25.____
     for the above paragraph is
         A. THE EVALUATION OF FORMULATED STANDARDS
         B. THE ATTRIBUTES OF SATISFACTORY STANDARDS
         C. THE ADOPTION OF ACCEPTABLE STANDARDS
         D. THE USE OF PROCESS OR PRODUCT STANDARDS

KEY (CORRECT ANSWERS)

TEST 1	TEST 2	TEST 3
1. C	1. B	1. B
2. C	2. A	2. A
3. D	3. C	3. E
4. A	4. C	4. D
5. B	5. A	5. E
6. D	6. D	6. C
7. C	7. A	7. A
8. A	8. C	8. D
9. D	9. D	9. A
10. D	10. B	10. C
11. B	11. C	11. D
12. C	12. A	12. C
13. A	13. D	13. B
14. A	14. D	14. A
15. C	15. B	15. C
16. B	16. C	16. B
17. C	17. C	17. C
18. B	18. B	18. C
19. A	19. D	19. B
20. B	20. D	20. A
21. A	21. D	21. D
22. C	22. B	22. C
23. B	23. D	23. D
24. D	24. C	24. A
25. B	25. B	25. B

EXAMINATION SECTION
TEST 1

DIRECTIONS: In each of the following questions, only one of the four sentences conforms to standards of correct usage. The other three contain errors in grammar, diction, or punctuation. Select the choice in each question which BEST conforms to standards of correct usage. Consider a choice correct if it contains none of the errors mentioned above, even though there may be other ways of expressing the same thought. *PRINT THE LETTER OF THE CORRECT ANSWER IN THE SPACE·AT THE RIGHT.*

1. A. Because he was ill was no excuse for his behavior.   1.___
    B. I insist that he see a lawyer before he goes to trial.
    C. He said "that he had not intended to go."
    D. He wasn't out of the office only three days.

2. A. He came to the station and pays a porter to carry his   2.___
       bags into the train.
    B. I should have liked to live in medieval times.
    C. My father was born in Linville. A little country town
       where everyone knows everyone else.
    D. The car, which is parked across the street, is disabled.

3. A. He asked the desk clerk for a clean, quiet, room.   3.___
    B. I expected James to be lonesome and that he would want
       to go home.
    C. I have stopped worrying because I have heard nothing
       further on the subject.
    D. If the board of directors controls the company, they
       may take actions which are disapproved by the stock-
       holders.

4. A. Each of the players knew their place.   4.___
    B. He whom you saw on the stage is the son of an actor.
    C. Susan is the smartest of the twin sisters.
    D. Who ever thought of him winning both prizes?

5. A. An outstanding trait of early man was their reliance   5.___
       on omens.
    B. Because I had never been there before.
    C. Neither Mr. Jones nor Mr. Smith has completed his work.
    D. While eating my dinner, a dog came to the window.

6. A. A copy of the lease, in addition to the Rules and   6.___
       Regulations, are to be given to each tenant.
    B. The Rules and Regulations and a copy of the lease is
       being given to each tenant.
    C. A copy of the lease, in addition to the Rules and
       Regulations, is to be given to each tenant.
    D. A copy of the lease, in addition to the Rules and
       Regulations, are being given to each tenant.

7. A. Although we understood that for him music was a
      passion, we were disturbed by the fact that he was
      addicted to sing along with the soloists.
   B. Do you believe that Steven is liable to win a scholar-
      ship?
   C. Give the picture to whomever is a connoisseur of art.
   D. Whom do you believe to be the most efficient worker in
      the office?   7.___

8. A. Each adult who is sure they know all the answers will
      some day realize their mistake.
   B. Even the most hardhearted villain would have to feel
      bad about so horrible a tragedy.
   C. Neither being licensed teachers, both aspirants had to
      pass rigorous tests before being appointed.
   D. The principal reason why he wanted to be designated
      was because he had never before been to a convention.   8.___

9. A. Being that the weather was so inclement, the party
      has been postponed for at least a month.
   B. He is in New York City only three weeks and he has
      already seen all the thrilling sights in Manhattan
      and in the other four boroughs.
   C. If you will look it up in the official directory,
      which can be consulted in the library during specified
      hours, you will discover that the chairman and director
      are Mr. T. Henry Long.
   D. Working hard at college during the day and at the post
      office during the night, he appeared to his family to
      be indefatigable.   9.___

10. A. I would have been happy to oblige you if you only
       asked me to do it.
    B. The cold weather, as well as the unceasing wind and
       rain, have made us decide to spend the winter in
       Florida.
    C. The politician would have been more successful in win-
       ning office if he would have been less dogmatic.
    D. These trousers are expensive; however, they will wear
       well.   10.___

11. A. All except him wore formal attire at the reception
       for the ambassador.
    B. If that chair were to be blown off of the balcony, it
       might injure someone below.
    C. Not a passenger, who was in the crash, survived the
       impact.
    D. To borrow money off friends is the best way to lose
       them.   11.___

12. A. Approaching Manhattan on the ferry boat from Staten
       Island, an unforgettable sight of the skyscrapers is
       seen.
    B. Did you see the exhibit of modernistic paintings as yet?
    C. Gesticulating wildly and ranting in stentorian tones,
       the speaker was the sinecure of all eyes.
    D. The airplane with crew and passengers was lost some-
       where in the Pacific Ocean.   12.___

13. A. If one has consistently had that kind of training, it   13.___
       is certainly too late to change your entire method of
       swimming long distances.
    B. The captain would have been more impressed if you
       would have been more conscientious in evacuation drills.
    C. The passangers on the stricken ship were all ready to
       abandon it at the signal.
    D. The villainous shark lashed at the lifeboat with it's
       tail, trying to upset the rocking boat in order to
       partake of it's contents.

14. A. As one whose been certified as a professional engineer,   14.___
       I belive that the decision to build a bridge over that
       harbor is unsound.
    B. Between you and me, this project ought to be completed
       long before winter arrives.
    C. He fervently hoped that the men would be back at camp
       and to find them busy at their usual chores.
    D. Much to his surprise, he discovered that the climate
       of Korea was like his home town.

15. A. An industrious executive is aided, not impeded, by   15.___
       having a hobby which gives him a fresh point of view
       on life and its problems.
    B. Frequent absence during the calendar year will surely
       mitigate against the chances of promotion.
    C. He was unable to go to the comittee meeting because he
       was very ill.
    D. Mr. Brown expressed his disapproval so emphatically
       that his associates were embarassed.

16. A. At our next session, the office manager will have told   16.___
       you something about his duties and responsibilities.
    B. In general, the book is absorbing and original and
       have no hesitation about recommending it.
    C. The procedures followed by private industry in dealing
       with lateness and absence are different from ours.
    D. We shall treat confidentially any information about
       Mr. Doe, to whom we understand you have sent reports
       to for many years.

17. A. I talked to one official, whom I knew was fully   17.___
       impartial.
    B. Everyone signed the petition but him.
    C. He proved not only to be a good student but also a
       good athlete.
    D. All are incorrect.

18. A. Every year a large amount of tenants are admitted to   18.___
       housing projects.
    B. Henry Ford owned around a billion dollars in indus-
       trial equipment.
    C. He was aggravated by the child's bead behavior.
    D. All are incorrect.

19. A. Before he was committed to the asylum he suffered
        from the illusion that he was Napoleon.
     B. Besides stocks, there were also bonds in the safe.
     C. We bet the other team easily.
     D. All are incorrect.

19.___

20. A. Bring this report to your supervisor immediately.
     B. He set the chair down near the table.
     C. The capitol of New York is Albany.
     D. All are incorrect.

20.___

21. A. He was chosen to arbitrate the dispute because every-
        one knew he would be disinterested.
     B. It is advisable to obtain the best council before
        making an important decision.
     C. Less college students are interested in teaching than
        ever before.
     D. All are incorrect.

21.___

22. A. She, hearing a signal, the source lamp flashed.
     B. While hearing a signal, the source lamp flashed.
     C. In hearing a signal, the source lamp flashed.
     D. As she heard a signal, the source lamp flashed.

22.___

23. A. Every one of the time records have been initialed in
        the designated spaces.
     B. All of the time records has been initialed in the
        designated spaces.
     C. Each one of the time records was initialed in the
        designated spaces.
     D. The time records all been initialed in the designated
        spaces.

23.___

24. A. If there is no one else to answer the phone, you will
        have to answer it.
     B. You will have to answer it yourself if no one else
        answers the phone.
     C. If no one else is not around to pick up the phone, you
        will have to do it.
     D. You will have to answer the phone when nobodys here to
        do it.

24.___

25. A. Dr. Barnes not in his office. What could I do for
        you?
     B. Dr. Barnes is not in his office. Is there something
        I can do for you?
     C. Since Dr. Barnes is not in his office, might there be
        something I may do for you?
     D. Is there any ways I can assist you since Dr. Barnes
        is not in his office?

25.___

26. A. She do not understand how the new console works.
     B. The way the new console works, she doesn't understand.
     C. She doesn't understand how the new console works.
     D. The new console works, so that she doesn't understand.

26.___

27. A. Certain changes in family income must be reported as they occur.
     B. When certain changes in family income occur, it must be reported.
     C. Certain family income changes must be reported as they occur.
     D. Certain changes in family income must be reported as they have been occuring.

27.___

28. A. Each tenant has to complete the application themselves.
     B. Each of the tenants have to complete the application by himself.
     C. Each of the tenants has to complete the application himself.
     D. Each of the tenants has to complete the application by themselves.

28.___

29. A. Yours is the only building that the construction will effect.
     B. Your's is the only building affected by the construction.
     C. The construction will only effect your building.
     D. Yours is the only building that will be affected by the construction.

29.___

30. A. There is four tests left.
     B. The number of tests left are four.
     C. There are four tests left.
     D. Four of the tests remains.

30.___

31. A. Each of the applicants takes a test.
     B. Each of the applicants take a test.
     C. Each of the applicants take tests.
     D. Each of the applicants have taken tests.

31.___

32. A. The applicant, not the examiners, are ready.
     B. The applicants, not the examiner, is ready.
     C. The applicants, not the examiner, are ready.
     D. The applicant, not the examiner, are ready.

32.___

33. A. You will not progress except you practice.
     B. You will not progress without you practicing.
     C. You will not progress unless you practice.
     D. You will not progress provided you do not practice.

33.___

34. A. Neither the director or the employees will be at the office tomorrow.
     B. Neither the director nor the employees will be at the office tomorrow.
     C. Neither the director, or the secretary nor the other employees will be at the office tomorrow.
     D. Neither the director, the secretary or the other employees will be at the office tomorrow.

34.___

35. A. In my absence he and her will have to finish the
      assignment.
    B. In my absence he and she will have to finish the
      assignment.
    C. In my absence she and him, they will have to finish
      the assignment.
    D. In my absence he and her both will have to finish the
      assignment.

35.____

KEY (CORRECT ANSWERS)

1. B	11. A	21. A	31. A
2. B	12. D	22. D	32. C
3. C	13. C	23. C	33. C
4. B	14. B	24. A	34. B
5. C	15. A	25. B	35. B
6. C	16. C	26. C	
7. D	17. B	27. A	
8. B	18. D	28. C	
9. D	19. B	29. D	
10. D	20. B	30. C	

TEST 2

Questions 1-4.

DIRECTIONS: Questions 1 through 4 consist of three sentences each. For each question, select the sentence which contains NO error in grammar or usage.

1. A. Be sure that everybody brings his notes to the con-   1.___
       ference.
    B. He looked like he meant to hit the boy.
    C. Mr. Jones is one of the clients who was chosen to
       represent the district
    D. All are incorrect.

2. A. He is taller than I.   2.___
    B. I'll have nothing to do with these kind of people.
    C. The reason why he will not buy the house is because it
       is too expensive.
    D. All are incorrect.

3. A. Aren't I eligible for this apartment.   3.___
    B. Have you seen him anywheres?
    C. He should of come earlier.
    D. All are incorrect.

4. A. He graduated college in 1982.   4.___
    B. He hadn't but one more line to write.
    C. Who do you think is the author of this report?
    D. All are incorrect.

Questions 5-35.

DIRECTIONS: In each of the following questions, only one of the four sentences conforms to standards of correct usage. The other three contain errors in grammar, diction, or punctuation. Select the choice in each question which BEST conforms to standards of correct usage. Consider a choice correct if it contains none of the errors mentioned above, even though there may be other ways of expressing the same thought.

5. A. It is obvious that no one wants to be a kill-joy if   5.___
       they can help it.
    B. It is not always possible, and perhaps it never is
       possible, to judge a person's character by just looking
       at him.

  C. When Yogi Berra of the New York Yankees hit an immortal grand-slam home run, everybody in the huge stadium including Pittsburgh fans, rose to his feet.

  D. Every one of us students must pay tuition today.

6. A. The physician told the young mother that if the baby 6.___
is not able to digest its milk, it should be boiled.

  B. There is no doubt whatsoever that he felt deeply hurt because John Smith had betrayed the trust.

  C. Having partaken of a most delicious repast prepared by Tessie Breen, the hostess, the horses were driven home immediately thereafter.

  D. The attorney asked my wife and myself several questions.

7. A. Despite all denials, there is no doubt in my mind that 7.___
if my father were here you wouldn't talk like that.

  B. At this time everyone must deprecate the demogogic attack made by one of our Senators on one of our most revered statesmen.

  C. In the first game of a crucial two-game series, Ted Williams, got two singles, both of them driving in a run.

  D. Our visitor brought good news to John and I.

8. A. If he would have told me, I should have been glad to 8.___
help him in his dire financial emergency.

  B. Newspaper men have often asserted that diplomats or so-called official spokesmen sometimes employ equivocation in attempts to deceive.

  C. I think someones coming to collect money for the Red Cross.

  D. In a masterly summation, the young attorney expressed his belief that the facts clearly militate aginst this opinion.

9. A. We have seen most all the exhibits. 9.___

  B. Without in the least underestimating your advice, in my opinion the situation has grown immeasurably worse in the past few days.

  C. I wrote to the box office treasurer of the hit show that a pair of orchestra seats would be preferable.

  D. As the grim story of Pearl Harbor was broadcast on that fateful December 7, it was the general opinion that war was inevitable.

10. A. Without a moment's hesitation, Casey Stengel said that 10.___
Larry Berra works harder than any player on the team.

  B. There is ample evidence to indicate that many animals can run faster than any human being.

  C. No one saw the accident but I.

  D. Example of courage is the heroic defense put up by the paratroopers against overwhelming odds.

11. A. If you prefer these kind, Mrs. Grey, we shall be more   11.___
        than willing to let you have them reasonably.
     B. If you like these here, Mrs. Grey, we shall be more
        than willing to let you have them reasonably.
     C. If you like these, Mrs. Grey, we shall be more than
        willing to let you have them.
     D. Who shall we appoint?

12. A. The number of errors are greater in speech than in   12.___
        writing.
     B. The doctor rather than the nurse was to blame for his
        being neglected.
     C. Because the demand for these books have been so great,
        we reduced the price.
     D. John Galsworthy, the English novelist, could not have
        survived a serious illness; had it not been for loving
        care.

13. A. Our activities this year have seldom ever been as   13.___
        interesting as they have been this month.
     B. Our activities this month have been more interesting,
        or at least as interesting as those of any month this
        year.
     C. Our activities this month has been more interesting
        than those of any other month this year.
     D. Neither Jean nor her sister was at home.

14. A. George B. Shaw's view of common morality, as well as   14.___
        his wit sparkling with a dash of perverse humor here
        and there, have led critics to term him "The Incurable
        Rebel."
     B. The President's program was not always received with
        the wholehearted endorsement of his own party, which is
        why the party faces difficulty in drawing up a platform
        for the coming election.
     C. The reason why they wanted to travel was because they
        had never been away from home.
     D. Facing a barrage of cameras, the visiting celebrity
        found it extremely difficult to express his opinions
        clearly.

15. A. When we calmed down, we all agreed that our anger had   15.___
        been kind of unnecessary and had not helped the
        situation.
     B. Without him going into all the details, he made us
        realize the horror of the accident.
     C. Like one girl, for example, who applied for two posi-
        tions.
     D. Do not think that you have to be so talented as he is
        in order to play in the school orchestra.

16. A. He looked very peculiarly to me.   16.___
     B. He certainly looked at me peculiar.
     C. Due to the train's being late, we had to wait an hour.
     D. The reason for the poor attendance is that it is
        raining.

17.
A. About one out of four own an automobile.
B. The collapse of the old Mitchell Bridge was caused by defective construction in the central pier.
C. Brooks Atkinson was well acquainted with the best literature, thus helping him to become an able critic.
D. He has to stand still until the relief man comes up, thus giving him no chance to move about and keep warm.

17.___

18.
A. He is sensitive to confusion and withdraws from people whom he feels are too noisy.
B. Do you know whether the data is statistically correct?
C. Neither the mayor or the aldermen are to blame:
D. Of those who were graduated from high school, a goodly percentage went to college.

18.___

19.
A. Acting on orders, the offices were searched by a designated committee.
B. The answer probably is nothing.
C. I thought it to be all right to excuse them from class.
D. I think that he is as successful a singer, if not more successful, than Mary.

19.___

20.
A. $120,000 is really very little to pay for such a well-built house.
B. The creatures looked like they had come from outer space.
C. It was her, he knew!
D. Nobody but me knows what to do.

20.___

21.
A. Mrs. Smith looked good in her new suit.
B. New York may be compared with Chicago.
C. I will not go to the meeting except you go with me.
D. I agree with this editorial.

21.___

22.
A. My opinions are different from his.
B. There will be less students in class now.
C. Helen was real glad to find her watch.
D. It had been pushed off of her dresser.

22.___

23.
A. Almost everone, who has been to California, returns with glowing reports.
B. George Washington, John Adams, and Thomas Jefferson, were our first presidents.
C. Mr. Walters, whom we met at the bank yesterday, is the man, who gave me my first job.
D. One should study his lessons as carefully as he can.

23.___

24.
A. We had such a good time yesterday.
B. When the bell rang, the boys and girls went in the schoolhouse.
C. John had the worst headache when he got up this morning.
D. Today's assignment is somewhat longer than yesterday's.

24.___

25. A. Neither the mayor nor the city clerk are willing to   25.___
       talk.
    B. Neither the mayor nor the city clerk is willing to
       talk.
    C. Neither the mayor or the city clerk are willing to talk.
    D. Neither the mayor or the city clerk is willing to talk.

26. A. Being that he is that kind of boy, cooperation cannot   26.___
       be expected.
    B. He interviewed people who he thought had something to
       say.
    C. Stop whomever enters the building regardless of rank or
       office held.
    D. Passing through the countryside, the scenery pleased us.

27. A. The childrens' shoes were in their closet.   27.___
    B. The children's shoes were in their closet.
    C. The childs' shoes were in their closet.
    D. The childs' shoes were in his closet.

28. A. An agreement was reached between the defendant, the   28.___
       plaintiff, the plaintiff's attorney and the insurance
       company as to the amount of the settlement.
    B. Everybody was asked to give their versions of the
       accident.
    C. The consensus of opinion was that the evidence was
       inconclusive.
    D. The witness stated that if he was rich, he wouldn't
       have had to loan the money.

29. A. Before beginning the investigation, all the materials   29.___
       relating to the case were carefully assembled.
    B. The reason for his inability to keep the appointment
       is because of his injury in the accident.
    C. This here evidence tends to support the claim of the
       defendant.
    D. We interviewed all the witnesses who, according to the
       driver, were still in town.

30. A. Each claimant was allowed the full amount of their   30.___
       medical expenses.
    B. Either of the three witnesses is available.
    C. Every one of the witnesses was asked to tell his story.
    D. Neither of the witnesses are right.

31. A. The commissioner, as well as his deputy and various   31.___
       bureau heads, were present.
    B. A new organization of employers and employees have
       been formed.
    C. One or the other of these men have been selected.
    D. The number of pages in the book is enough to discourage
       a reader.

32. A. Between you and me, I think he is the better man.   32.____
     B. He was believed to be me.
     C. Is it us that you wish to see?
     D. The winners are him and her.

33. A. Beside the statement to the police, the witness spoke   33.____
        to no one.
     B. He made no statement other than to the police and I.
     C. He made no statement to any one else, aside from the
        police.
     D. The witness spoke to no one but me.

34. A. The claimant has no one to blame but himself.   34.____
     B. The boss sent us, he and I, to deliver the packages.
     C. The lights come from mine and not his car.
     D. There was room on the stairs for him and myself.

35. A. Admission to this clinic is limited to patients'   35.____
        inability to pay for medical care.
     B. Patients who can pay little or nothing for medical care
        are treated in this clinic.
     C. The patient's ability to pay for medical care is the
        determining factor in his admissibility to this clinic.
     D. This clinic is for the patient's that cannot afford to
        pay or that can pay a little for medical care.

————

KEY (CORRECT ANSWERS)

1. A	11. C	21. A	31. D
2. A	12. B	22. A	32. A
3. D	13. D	23. D	33. D
4. C	14. D	24. D	34. A
5. D	15. D	25. B	35. B
6. D	16. D	26. B	
7. B	17. B	27. B	
8. B	18. D	28. C	
9. D	19. B	29. D	
10. B	20. D	30. C	

————

PREPARING WRITTEN MATERIALS
EXAMINATION SECTION

DIRECTIONS: Each of the two sentences in the following questions may contain errors in punctuation, capitalization, or grammar.
If there is an error in only Sentence I, mark your answer A.
If there is an error in only Sentence II, mark your answer B.
If there is an error in both Sentence I and Sentence II, mark your answer C.
If both Sentence I and Sentence II are correct, mark your answer D.

TEST 1

1. I. The task of typing these reports is to be divided equally between you and me.
    II. If I was he, I would use a different method for filing these records.   1.____

2. I. The new clerk is just as capable as some of the older employees, if not more capable.
    II. Using his knowledge of arithmetic to check the calculations, the supervisor found no errors in the report.   2.____

3. I. A typist who does consistently superior work probably merits promotion.
    II. In its report on the stenographic unit, the committee pointed out that neither the stenographers nor the typists were adequately trained.   3.____

4. I. Entering the office, the desk was noticed immediately by the visitor.
    II. Arrangements have been made to give this training to whoever applies for it.   4.____

5. I. The office manager estimates that this assignment, which is to be handled by you and I, will require about two weeks for completion.
    II. One of the recommendations of the report is that these kind of forms be discarded because they are of no value.   5.____

6. I. The supervisor knew that the typist was a quiet, cooperative, efficient, employee.
    II. The duties of a stenographer are to take dictation notes at conferences and transcribing them.   6.____

7. I. The stenographer has learned that she, as well as two typists, is being assigned to the new unit.
    II. We do not know who you have designated to take charge of the new program.   7.____

8. I. He asked, "When do you expect to return?"
    II. I doubt whether this system will be successful here; it is not suitable for the work of our agency.   8.____

9. I. It is a policy of this agency to encourage punctuality
        as a good habit for we employees to adopt.
    II. The successful completion of the task was due largely
        to them cooperating effectively with the supervisor.   9.___

10. I. Mr. Smith, who is a very competent executive has
       offered his services to our department.
    II. Every one of the stenographers who work in this office
        is considered trustworthy.   10.___

11. I. It is very annoying to have a pencil sharpener, which
       is not in proper working order.
    II. The building watchman checked the door of Charlie's
        office and found that the lock has been jammed.   11.___

12. I. Since he went on the New York City council a year
       ago, one of his primary concerns has been safety
       in the streets.
    II. After waiting in the doorway for about 15 minutes,
        a black sedan appeared.   12.___

13. I. When you are studying a good textbook is important.
    II. He said he would divide the money equally between
        you and me.   13.___

14. I. The question is, "How can a large number of envelopes
       be sealed rapidly without the use of a sealing
       machine?"
    II. The administrator assigned two stenographers, Mary
        and I, to the new bureau.   14.___

15. I. A dictionary, in addition to the office management
       textbooks, were placed on his desk.
    II. The concensus of opinion is that none of the employees
        should be required to work overtime.   15.___

16. I. Mr. Granger has demonstrated that he is as courageous,
       if not more courageous, than Mr. Brown.
    II. The successful completion of the project depends on
        the manager's accepting our advisory opinion.   16.___

17. I. Mr. Ames was in favor of issuing a set of rules and
       regulations for all of us employees to follow.
    II. It is inconceivable that the new clerk knows how to
        deal with that kind of correspondence.   17.___

18. I. The revised referrence manual is to be used by all
       of the employees.
    II. Mr. Johnson told Miss Kent and me to accumulate all
        the letters that we receive.   18.___

19. I. The supervisor said, that before any changes would be
       made in the attendance report, there must be ample
       justification for them.
    II. Each of them was asked to amend their preliminary
        report.   19.___

20.   I. Mrs. Peters conferred with Mr. Roberts before she   20.___
         laid the papers on his desk.
     II. As far as this report is concerned, Mr. Williams
         always has and will be responsible for its preparation.

———

KEY (CORRECT ANSWERS)

1.	B	11.	C
2.	D	12.	C
3.	D	13.	A
4.	A	14.	B
5.	C	15.	C
6.	C	16.	A
7.	B	17.	B
8.	D	18.	A
9.	C	19.	C
10.	A	20.	B

———

TEST 2

DIRECTIONS: Each question or incomplete statement is followed by several suggested answers or completions. Select the one that BEST answers the question or completes the statement. *PRINT THE LETTER OF THE CORRECT ANSWER IN THE SPACE AT THE RIGHT.*

Questions 1-9.

DIRECTIONS: Questions 1 through 9 consist of pairs of sentences which may or may not contain errors in grammar, capitalization, or punctuation.
If both sentences are correct, mark your answer A.
If the first sentence only is correct, mark your answer B.
If the second sentence only is correct, mark your answer C.
If both sentences are incorrect, mark your answer D.
NOTE: Consider a sentence correct if it contains no errors, although there may be other correct ways of writing the sentence.

1.   I. An unusual conference will be held today at George Washington high school.
   II. The principal of the school, Dr. Pace, described the meeting as "a unique opportunity for educators to exchange ideas."   1.___

2.   I. Studio D, which they would ordinarily use, will be occupied at that time.
   II. Any other studio, which is properly equipped, may be used instead.   2.___

3.   I. D.H. Lawrence's <u>Sons and Lovers</u> were discussed on today's program.
   II. Either Eliot's or Yeats's work is to be covered next week.   3.___

4.   I. This program is on the air for three years now, and has a well-established audience.
   II. We have received many complimentary letters from listeners, and scarcely no critical ones.   4.___

5.   I. Both Mr. Owen and Mr. Mitchell have addressed the group.
   II. As has Mr. Stone, whose talks have been especially well received.   5.___

6.   I. The original program was different in several respects from the version that eventually went on the air.
   II. Each of the three announcers who Mr. Scott thought had had suitable experience was asked whether he would be willing to take on the special assignment.   6.___

7. I. A municipal broadcasting system provides extensive   7.___
    coverage of local events, but also reports national
    and international news.
    II. A detailed account of happenings in the South may be
    carried by a local station hundreds of miles away.

8. I. Jack Doe the announcer and I will be working on the   8.___
    program.
    II. The choice of musical selections has been left up
    to he and I.

9. I. Mr. Taylor assured us that "he did not anticipate   9.___
    any difficulty in making arrangements for the broad-
    cast."
    II. Although there had seemed at first to be certain
    problems; these had been solved.

Questions 10-14.

DIRECTIONS: Questions 10 through 14 consist of pairs of sentences
which may contain errors in grammar, sentence structure,
punctuation, or spelling, or both sentences may be
correct. Consider a sentence correct if it contains
no errors, although there may be other correct ways of
writing the sentence.
If only Sentence I contains an error, mark your answer A.
If only Sentence II contains an error, mark your answer B.
If both sentences contain errors, mark your answer C.
If both sentences are correct, mark your answer D.

10. I. No employee considered to be indispensable will be   10.___
    assigned to the new office.
    II. The arrangement of the desks and chairs give the
    office a neat appearance.

11. I. The recommendation, accompanied by a report, was   11.___
    delivered this morning.
    II. Mr. Green thought the procedure would facilitate his
    work; he knows better now.

12. I. Limiting the term "property" to tangible property,   12.___
    in the criminal mischief setting, accords with prior
    case law holding that only tangible property came
    within the purview of the offense of malicious
    mischief.
    II. Thus, a person who intentionally destroys the property
    of another, but under an honest belief that he has
    title to such property, cannot be convicted of criminal
    mischief under the Revised Penal Law.

13. I. Very early in its history, New York enacted statutes   13.___
    from time to time punishing, either as a felony or
    as a misdemeanor, malicious injuries to various kinds
    of property: piers, booms, dams, bridges, etc.

II. The application of the statute is necessarily restricted to trespassory takings with larcenous intent: namely with intent permanently or virtually permanently to "appropriate" property or "deprive" the owner of its use.

14.   I. Since the former Penal Law did not define the instruments of forgery in a general fashion, its crime of forgery was held to be narrower than the common law offense in this respect and to embrace only those instruments explicitly specified in the substantive provisions.

    II. After entering the barn through an open door for the purpose of stealing, it was closed by the defendants.

14.____

Questions 15-20.

DIRECTIONS: Questions 15 through 20 consist of pairs of sentences which may or may not contain errors in grammar, capitalization, or punctuation.
If both sentences are correct, mark your answer A.
If the first sentence only is correct, mark your answer B.
If the second sentence only is correct, mark your answer C
If both sentences are incorrect, mark your answer D.
NOTE: Consider a sentence correct if it contains no errors, although there may be other correct ways of writing the sentence.

15.   I. The program, which is currently most popular, is a news broadcast.
    II. The engineer assured his supervisor that there was no question of his being late again.

15.____

16.   I. The announcer recommended that the program originally scheduled for that time be cancelled.
    II. Copies of the script may be given to whoever is interested.

16.____

17.   I. A few months ago it looked like we would be able to broadcast the concert live.
    II. The program manager, as well as the announcers, were enthusiastic about the plan.

17.____

18.   I. No speaker on the subject of education is more interesting than he.
    II. If he would have had the time, we would have scheduled him for a regular weekly broadcast.

18.____

19.   I. This quartet, in its increasingly complex variations on a simple theme, admirably illustrates Professor Baker's point.
    II. Listeners interested in these kind of ideas will find his recently published study of Haydn rewarding.

19.____

20.   I. The Commissioner's resignation at the end of next   20.___
        month marks the end of a long public service career.
   II. Outstanding among his numerous achievements were his
        successful implementation of several revolutionary
        schemes to reorganize the agency.

KEY (CORRECT ANSWERS)

1. C		11. D	
2. B		12. C	
3. C		13. B	
4. D		14. A	
5. B		15. C	
6. A		16. A	
7. A		17. D	
8. D		18. B	
9. D		19. B	
10. B		20. B	

RECORD KEEPING
EXAMINATION SECTION
TEST 1

DIRECTIONS: Each question or incomplete statement is followed by
several suggested answers or completions. Select the
one that BEST answers the question or completes the
statement. *PRINT THE LETTER OF THE CORRECT ANSWER IN
THE SPACE AT THE RIGHT.*

Questions 1-15.

DIRECTIONS: Questions 1 through 15 are to be answered on the basis
of the following list of company names below. Arrange
a file alphabetically, word-by-word, disregarding
punctuation, conjunctions, and apostrophes. Then
answer the questions.

        A Bee C Reading Materials
        ABCO Parts
        A Better Course for Test Preparation
        AAA Auto Parts Co.
        A-Z Auto Parts, Inc.
        Aabar Books
        Abbey, Joanne
        Boman-Sylvan Law Firm
        BMW Autowerks
        C Q Service Company
        Chappell-Murray, Inc.
        E&E Life Insurance
        Emcrisco
        Gigi Arts
        Gordon, Jon & Associates
        SOS Plumbing
        Schmidt, J.B. Co.

1. Which of these files should appear FIRST?   1.___
        A. ABCO Parts
        B. A Bee C Reading Materials
        C. A Better Course for Test Preparation
        D. AAA Auto Parts Co.

2. Which of these files should appear SECOND?   2.___
        A. A-Z Auto Parts, Inc.
        B. A Bee C Reading Materials
        C. A Better Course for Test Preparation
        D. AAA Auto Parts Co.

3. Which of these files should appear THIRD?   3.___
        A. ABCO Parts
        B. A Bee C Reading Materials
        C. Aabar Books
        D. AAA Auto Parts Co.

4. Which of these files should appear FOURTH? 4.___
   A. ABCO Parts
   B. A Bee C Reading Materials
   C. Abbey, Joanne
   D. AAA Auto Parts Co.

5. Which of these files should appear LAST? 5.___
   A. Gordon, Jon & Associates
   B. Gigi Arts
   C. Schmidt, J.B. Co.
   D. SOS Plumbing

6. Which of these files should appear between A-Z Auto Parts, 6.___
   Inc. and Abbey, Joanne?
   A. A Bee C Reading Materials
   B. AAA Auto Parts Co.
   C. Aabar Books
   D. A Better Course for Test Preparation

7. Which of these files should appear between ABCO Parts and 7.___
   Aabar Books?
   A. A Bee C Reading Materials
   B. Abbey, Joanne
   C. Aabar Books
   D. A-Z Auto Parts

8. Which of these files should appear between Abbey, Joanne 8.___
   and Boman-Sylvan Law Firm?
   A. A Better Course for Test Preparation
   B. BMW Autowerks
   C. A-Z Auto Parts,Inc.
   D. Aabar Books

9. Which of these files should appear between Abbey, Joanne 9.___
   and C Q Service?
   A. A-Z Auto Parts,Inc.   B. BMW Autowerks
   C. Choices A and B   D. Chappell-Murray, Inc.

10. Which of these files should appear between C Q Service 10.___
    Company and Emcrisco?
    A. Chappell-Murray,Inc.   B. E&E Life Insurance
    C. Gigi Arts   D. Choices A and B

11. Which of these files should NOT appear between C Q Service 11.___
    Company and E&E Life Insurance?
    A. Gordon, Jon & Associates
    B. Emcrisco
    C. Gigi Arts
    D. Choices A and C

12. Which of these files should appear between Chappell-Murray 12.___
    Inc., and Gigi Arts?
    A. CQ Service Inc.   E&E Life Insurance, and Emcrisco
    B. Emcrisco, E&E Life Insurance, and Gordon, Jon &
       Associates

C. E&E Life Insurance and Emcrisco
D. Emcrisco and Gordon, Jon & Associates

13. Which of these files should appear between Gordon, Jon & Associates and SOS Plumbing? 13.___
 A. Gigi Arts   B. Schmidt, J.B. Co.
 C. Choices A and B   D. None of the above

14. Which of the choices lists the four files in their proper alphabetical order? 14.___
 A. E&E Life Insurance; Gigi Arts; Gordon, Jon & Associates; SOS Plumbing
 B. E&E Life Insurance; Emcrisco; Gigi Arts; SOS Plumbing
 C. Emcrisco; Gordon, Jon & Associates; Schmidt, J.B. Co.; SOS Plumbing
 D. Emcrisco; Gigi Arts; Gordon, Jon & Associates; SOS Plumbing

15. Which of the choices lists the four files in their proper alphabetical order? 15.___
 A. Gigi Arts; Gordon, Jon & Associates; SOS Plumbing; Schmidt, J.B. Co.
 B. Gordon, Jon & Associates; Gigi Arts; Schmidt, J.B. Co.; SOS Plumbing
 C. Gordon, Jon & Associates; Gigi Arts; SOS Plumbing; Schmidt, J.B. Co.
 D. Gigi Arts; Gordon, Jon & Associates; Schmidt, J.B. Co.; SOS Plumbing

16. The alphabetical filing order of two businesses with identical names is determined by the 16.___
 A. length of time each business has been operating
 B. addresses of the businesses
 C. last name of the company president
 D. none of the above

17. In an alphabetical filing system, if a business name includes a number, it should be 17.___
 A. disregarded
 B. considered a number and placed at the end of an alphabetical section
 C. treated as though it were written in words and alphabetized accordingly
 D. considered a number and placed at the beginning of an alphabetical section

18. If a business name includes a contraction (such as *don't* or *it's*), how should that word be treated in an alphabetical filing system? 18.___
 A. Divide the word into its separate parts and treat it as two words.
 B. Ignore the letters that come after the apostrophe.
 C. Ignore the word that contains the contraction.
 D. Ignore the apostrophe and consider all letters in the contraction.

19. In what order should the parts of an address be considered 19.___
    when using an alphabetical filing system?
    - A. City or town; state; street name; house or building number
    - B. State; city or town; street name; house or building number
    - C. House or building number; street name; city or town; state
    - D. Street name; city or town; state

20. A business record should be cross-referenced when a(n) 20.___
    - A. organization is known by an abbreviated name
    - B. business has a name change because of a sale, incorporation, or other reason
    - C. business is known by a *coined* or common name which differs from a dictionary spelling
    - D. all of the above

21. A geographical filing system is MOST effective when 21.___
    - A. location is more important than name
    - B. many names or titles sound alike
    - C. dealing with companies who have offices all over the world
    - D. filing personal and business files

Questions 22-25.

DIRECTIONS: Questions 22 through 25 are to be answered on the basis of the list of items below, which are to be filed geographically. Organize the items geographically and then answer the questions.

    1. University Press at Berkeley, U.S.
    2. Maria Sanchez, Mexico City, Mexico
    3. Great Expectations Ltd. in London, England
    4. Justice League, Cape Town, South Africa, Africa
    5. Crown Pearls Ltd. in London, England
    6. Joseph Prasad in London, England

22. Which of the following arrangements of the items is 22.___
    composed according to the policy of: *Continent, Country, City, Firm or Individual Name*?
    - A. 5, 3, 4, 6, 2, 1   B. 4, 5, 3, 6, 2, 1
    - C. 1, 4, 5, 3, 6, 2   D. 4, 5, 3, 6, 1, 2

23. Which of the following files is arranged according to 23.___
    the policy of: *Continent, Country, City, Firm or Individual Name*?
    - A. South Africa. Africa. Cape Town. Justice League
    - B. Mexico. Mexico City. Maria Sanchez
    - C. North America. United States. Berkeley. University Press
    - D. England. Europe. London. Prasad, Joseph

24. Which of the following arrangements of the items is composed according to the policy of: *Country, City, Firm or Individual Name*?
    A. 5, 6, 3, 2, 4, 1   B. 1, 5, 6, 3, 2, 4
    C. 6, 5, 3, 2, 4, 1   D. 5, 3, 6, 2, 4, 1

24.___

25. Which of the following files is arranged according to a policy of: *Country, City, Firm or Individual Name*?
    A. England. London. Crown Pearls Ltd.
    B. North America. United States. Berkeley. University Press
    C. Africa. Cape Town. Justice League
    D. Mexico City. Mexico. Maria Sanchez

25.___

26. Under which of the following circumstances would a phonetic filing system be MOST effective?
    A. When the person in charge of filing can't spell very well
    B. With large files with names that sound alike
    C. With large files with names that are spelled alike
    D. All of the above

26.___

Questions 27-29.

DIRECTIONS: Questions 27 through 29 are to be answered on the basis of the following list of numerical files.

    1. 391-023-100
    2. 361-132-170
    3. 385-732-200
    4. 381-432-150
    5. 391-632-387
    6. 361-423-303
    7. 391-123-271

27. Which of the following arrangements of the files follows a consecutive-digit system?
    A. 2, 3, 4, 1   B. 1, 5, 7, 3
    C. 2, 4, 3, 1   D. 3, 1, 5, 7

27.___

28. Which of the following arrangements follows a terminal-digit system?
    A. 1, 7, 2, 4, 3   B. 2, 1, 4, 5, 7
    C. 7, 6, 5, 4, 3   D. 1, 4, 2, 3, 7

28.___

29. Which of the following lists follows a middle-digit system?
    A. 1, 7, 2, 6, 4, 5, 3   B. 1, 2, 7, 4, 6, 5, 3
    C. 7, 2, 1, 3, 5, 6, 4   D. 7, 1, 2, 4, 6, 5, 3

29.___

Questions 30-31.

DIRECTIONS: Questions 30 and 31 are to be answered on the basis
             of the following information.

1. Reconfirm Laura Bates appointment with James Caldecort
    on December 12 at 9:30 A.M.
2. Laurence Kinder contact Julia Lucas on August 3 and set
    up a meeting for week of September 23 at 4 P.M.
3. John Lutz contact Larry Waverly on August 3 and set up
    appointment for September 23 at 9:30 A.M.
4. Call for tickets for Gerry Stanton August 21 for New
    Jersey on September 23, flight 143 at 4:43 P.M.

30. A chronological file for the above information would be   30.___
     A. 4, 3, 2, 1   B. 3, 2, 4, 1
     C. 4, 2, 3, 1   D. 3, 1, 2, 4

31. Using the above information, a chronological file for the   31.___
     date of September 23 would be
     A. 2, 3, 4   B. 3, 1, 4   C. 3, 2, 4   D. 4, 3, 2

Questions 32-34.

DIRECTIONS: Questions 32 through 34 are to be answered on the
             basis of the following information.

1. Call Roger Epstein, Ashoke Naipaul, Jon Anderson, and
    Sarah Washington on April 19 at 1:00 P.M. to set up
    meeting with Alika D'Ornay for June 6 in New York
2. Call Martin Ames before noon on April 19 to confirm
    afternoon meeting with Bob Greenwood on April 20th
3. Set up meeting room at noon for 2:30 P.M. meeting on
    April 19th
4. Ashley Stanton contact Bob Greenwood at 9:00 A.M. on
    April 20 and set up meeting for June 6 at 8:30 A.M.
5. Carol Guiland contact Shelby Van Ness during afternoon
    of April 20 and set up meeting for June 6 at 10:00 A.M.
6. Call airline and reserve tickets on June 6 for
    Roger Epstein trip to Denver on July 8
7. Meeting at 2:30 P.M. on April 19th

32. A chronological file for all of the above information   32.___
     would be
     A. 2, 1, 3, 7, 5, 4, 6   B. 3, 7, 2, 1, 4, 5, 6
     C. 3, 7, 1, 2, 5, 4, 6   D. 2, 3, 1, 7, 4, 5, 6

33. A chronological file for the date of April 19th would be   33.___
     A. 2, 3, 7, 1   B. 2, 3, 1, 7
     C. 7, 1, 3, 2   D. 3, 7, 1, 2

34. Add the following information to the file, and then   34.___
    create a chronological file for April 20th:
    8. April 20: 3:00 P.M. meeting between Bob Greenwood
    and Martin Ames.
       A. 4, 5, 8   B. 4, 8, 5   C. 8, 5, 4   D. 5, 4, 8

35. The PRIMARY advantage of computer records filing over   35.___
    a manual system is
       A. speed of retrieval   B. accuracy
       C. cost   D. potential file loss

___

KEY (CORRECT ANSWERS)

1. B	11. B	21. A	31. C
2. C	12. C	22. B	32. D
3. D	13. D	23. C	33. B
4. A	14. D	24. D	34. A
5. C	15. A	25. A	35. A
6. C	16. B	26. B	
7. D	17. C	27. C	
8. B	18. D	28. D	
9. B	19. A	29. A	
10. D	20. D	30. B	

___

BASIC FUNDAMENTALS OF
FILING SCIENCE

I. COMMENTARY

Filing is the systematic arrangement and storage of papers, cards, forms, catalogues, etc., so that they may be found easily and quickly. The importance of an efficient filing system cannot be emphasized too strongly. The filed materials form records which may be needed quickly to settle questions that may cause embarrassing situations if such evidence is not available. In addition to keeping papers in order so that they are readily available. the filing system must also be designed to keep papers in good condition. A filing system must be planned so that papers may be filed easily, withdrawn easily, and as quickly returned to their proper place. The cost of a filing system is also an important factor.

The need for a filing system arose when the business man began to carry on negotiations on a large scale. He could no longer be intimate with the details of his business. What was needed in the early era was a spindle or pigeon-hole desk. Filing in pigeon-hole desks is now almost completely extinct. It was an unsatisfactory practice since pigeon holes were not labeled, and the desk was an untidy mess.

II. BASIS OF FILING

The science of filing is an exact one and entails a thorough understanding of basic facts, materials, and methods. An overview of this important information now follows.

   1. <u>Types of files</u>

      (1) SHANNON FILE

This consists of a board, at one end of which are fastened two arches which may be opened laterally.

      (2) SPINDLE FILE

This consists of a metal or wood base to which is attached a long, pointed spike. Papers are pushed down on the spike as received. This file is useful for temporary retention of papers.

      (3) BOX FILE

This is a heavy cardboard or metal box, opening from the side like a book.

      (4) FLAT FILE

This consists of a series of shallow drawers or trays, arranged like drawers in a cabinet.

      (5) BELLOWS FILE

This is a heavy cardboard container with alphabetized or compartment sections, the ends of which are closed in such a manner that they resemble an accordion.

      (6) VERTICAL FILE

This consists of one or more drawers in which the papers are stood on edge, usually in folders, and are indexed by guides. A series of two or more drawers in one unit is the usual file cabinet.

      (7) CLIP FILE

This file has a large clip attached to a board and is very similar to the *SHANNON FILE*.

      (8) VISIBLE FILE

Cards are filed flat in an overlapping arrangement which leaves a part of each card visible at all times.

(9) ROTARY FILE

The *ROTARY FILE* has a number of visible card files attached to a post around which they can be revolved. The wheel file has visible cards which rotate around a horizontal axle.

(10) TICKLER FILE

This consists of cards or folders marked with the days of the month, in which materials are filed and turned up on the appropriate day of the month.

2. <u>Aids in filing</u>

(1) GUIDES

Guides are heavy cardboard, pasteboard, or bristol-board sheets the same size as folders. At the top is a tab on which is marked or printed the distinguishing letter, words, or numbers indicating the material filed in a section of the drawer.

(2) SORTING TRAYS

Sorting trays are equipped with alphabetical guides to facilitate the sorting of papers preparatory to placing them in a file.

(3) CODING

Once the classification or indexing caption has been de-termined, it must be indicated on the letter for filing purposes.

(4) CROSS REFERENCE

Some letters or papers might easily be called for under two or more captions. For this purpose, a cross-reference card or sheet is placed in the folder or in the index.

3. <u>Variations of filing systems</u>

(1) VARIADEX ALPHABETIC INDEX

Provides for more effective expansion of the alphabetic system.

(2) TRIPLE-CHECK NUMERIC FILING

Entails a multiple cross-reference, as the name implies.

(3) VARIADEX FILING

Makes use of color as an aid in filing.

(4) DEWEY DECIMAL SYSTEM

The system is a numeric one used in libraries or for filing library materials in an office. This special type of filing system is used where material is grouped in finely divi-ded categories, such as in libraries. With this method, all ma-terial to be filed is divided into ten major groups, from 000 to 900, and then subdivided into tens, units, and decimals.

4. <u>Centralized filing</u>

Centralized filing means keeping the files in one specific or central location. Decentralized filing means putting away papers in files of individual departments. The first step in the organization of a central filing department is to make a careful canvass of all desks in the offices. In this manner we can determine just what material needs to be filed, and what information each desk occupant requires from the central file. Only papers which may be used at some time by persons in the various offices should be placed in the central file. A paper that is to be used at some time by persons in the various of-fices should be placed in the central file. A paper that is to be used by one department only should never be filed in the cen-tral file.

5. Methods of filing

While there are various methods used for filing, actually there are only five basic systems: alphabetical, subject, numerical, geographic, and chronological. All other systems are derived from one of these or from a combination of two or more of them.

Since the purpose of a filing system is to store business records systemically so that any particular record can be found almost instantly when required, filing requires, in addition to the proper kinds of equipment and supplies, an effective method of indexing.

There are five basic systems of filing:

(1) ALPHABETIC FILING

Most filing is alphabetical. Other methods, as described below, require extensive alphabetization.

In alphabetic filing, lettered dividers or guides are arranged in alphabetic sequence. Material to be filed is placed behind the proper guide. All materials under each letter are also arranged alphabetically. Folders are used unless the file is a card index.

(2) SUBJECT FILING

This method is used when a single, complete file on a certain subject is desired. A subject file is often maintained to assemble all correspondence on a certain subject. Such files are valuable in connection with insurance claims, contract negotiations, personnel, and other investigations, special programs, and similar subjects.

(3) GEOGRAPHICAL FILE

Materials are filed according to location: states, cities, counties, or other subdivisions. Statistics and tax information are often filed in this manner.

(4) CHRONOLOGICAL FILE

Records are filed according to date. This method is used especially in "tickler" files that have guides numbered 1 to 31 for each day of the month. Each number indicates the day of the month when the filed item requires attention.

(5) NUMERICAL FILE

This method requires an alphabetic card index giving name and number. The card index is used to locate records numbered consecutively in the files according to date received or sequence in which issued, such as licenses, permits, etc.

6. Indexing

Determining the name or title under which an item is to be filed is known as indexing. For example, how would a letter from Robert E. Smith be filed? The name would be rearranged Smith, Robert E., so that the letter would be filed under the last name.

7. Alphabetizing

The arranging of names for filing is known as alphabetizing. For example, suppose you have four letters indexed under the names Johnson, Becker, Roe, and Stern. How should these letters be arranged in the files so that they may be found easily? You would arrange the four names alphabetically, thus, Becker, Johnson, Roe, and Stern.

III. RULES FOR INDEXING AND ALPHABETIZING

1. The names of persons are to be transposed. Write the surname first, then the given name, and, finally, the middle name or initial. Then arrange the various names according to the alphabetic order of letters throughout the entire name. If there is a title, consider that after the middle name or initial.

NAMES	*INDEXED AS*
Arthur L. Bright	Bright, Arthur L.
Arthur S. Bright	Bright, Arthur S.
P.E. Cole	Cole, P.E.
Dr. John C. Fox	Fox, John C. (Dr.)

2. If a surname includes the same letters of another surname, with one or more additional letters added to the end, the shorter surname is placed first regardless of the given name or the initial of the given name.

NAMES	*INDEXED AS*
Robert E. Brown	Brown, Robert E.
Gerald A. Browne	Browne, Gerald A.
William O. Brownell	Brownell, William O.

3. Firm names are alphabetized under the surnames. Words like the, an, a, of, and for, are not considered.

NAMES	*INDEXED AS*
Bank of America	Bank of America
Bank Discount Dept.	Bank Discount Dept.
The Cranford Press	Cranford Press, The
Nelson Dwyer & Co.	Dwyer, Nelson, & Co.
Sears, Roebuck & Co.	Sears, Roebuck & Co.
Montgomery Ward & Co.	Ward, Montgomery, & Co.

4. The order of filing is determined first of all by the first letter of the names to be filed. If the first letters are the same, the order is determined by the second letters, and so on. In the following pairs of names, the order is determined by the letters underlined:

A̲usten	H̲ayes	Ha̲nson	Har̲vey	Heath̲	Gree̲n	Schwart̲z
B̲aker	H̲eath	Ha̲rper	Har̲wood	Heato̲n	Gree̲ne	Schwar̲z

5. When surnames are unlike, those with initials only precede those with given names, unless the first initial comes alphabetically after the first letter of the name.

Gleason, S.	*but,*	Abbot, Mary
Gleason, S.W.		Abbott, W.B.
Gleason, Sidney		

6. Hyphenated names are treated as if spelled without the hyphen.

Lloyd-Jones, James	Lloyd, Robert
Lloyd, Paul N.	Lloyd-Thomas, A.S.

7. Company names composed of single letters which are not used as abbreviations precede the other names beginning with the same letter.

B & S Garage	E Z Duplicator Co.
B X Cable Co.	Eagle Typewriter Co.
Babbitt, R.N.	Edison Company

8. The ampersand (&) and the apostrophe (') in firm names are disregarded in alphabetizing.

Nelson & Niller	M & C Amusement Corp.
Nelson, Walter J.	M C Art Assn.
Nelson's Bakery	

9. Names beginning with Mac, Mc, or M' are usually placed in regular order as spelled. Some filing systems file separately names beginning with Mc.

    MacDonald, R.J.   Mazza, Anthony
    Macdonald, S.B.   McAdam, Wm.
    Mace, Wm.   McAndrews, Jerry

10. Names beginning with St. are listed as if the name Saint were spelled in full. Numbered street names and all abbreviated names are treated as if spelled out in full.

Saginaw	Fifth Avenue Hotel	Hart Mfg. Co.
St. Louis	42nd Street Dress Shop	Hart, Martin
St. Peter's Rectory	Hart, Chas.	Hart, Thos.
Sandford	Hart, Charlotte	Hart, Thomas A.
Smith, Wm.	Hart, Jas.	Hart, Thos. R.
Smith, Willis	Hart, Janice	

11. Federal, state, or city departments of government should be placed alphabetically under the governmental branch controlling them.

    Illinois, State of -- Departments and Commissions
        Banking Dept.
        Employment Bureau
    United States Government Departments
        Commerce
        Defense
        State
        Treasury

12. Alphabetic order
    Each word in a name is an indexing unit. Arrange the names in alphabetic order by comparing similar units in each name. Consider the second units only when the first units are identical. Consider the third units only when both the first and second units are identical.

13. Single surnames or initials
    A surname, when used alone, precedes the same surname with a first name or initial. A surname with a first initial only precedes a surname with a complete first name. This rule is sometimes stated, "nothing comes before something."

14. Surname prefixes
    A surname prefix is not a separate indexing unit, but it is considered part of the surname. These prefixes include: d', D', Da, de, De, Del, Des, Di, Du, Fitz., La, Le, Mc, Mac, 'c, O', St., Van, Van der, Von, Von der, and others. The prefixes M', Mac, and Mc are indexed and filed exactly as they are spelled.

15. Names of firms
    Names of firms and institutions are indexed and filed exactly as they are written when they do not contain the complete name of an individual.

16. Names of firms containing complete individual names
    When the firm or institution name includes the complete name of an individual, the units are transposed for indexing in the same way as the name of an individual.

17. Article "The"
    When the article the occurs at the beginning of a name, it is placed at the end in parentheses but it is not moved. In both cases, it is not an indexing unit and is disregarded in filing.

18. Hyphenated names
    Hyphenated firm names are considered as separate indexing units. Hyphenated surnames of individuals are considered as one indexing unit; this applies also to hyphenated names of individuals whose complete names are part of a firm name.

19. Abbreviations

Abbreviations are considered as though the name were written in full; however, single letters other than abbreviations are considered as separate indexing units.

20. Conjunctions, prepositions and firm endings

Conjunctions and prepositions, such as and, for, in, of, are disregarded in indexing and filing but are not omitted or their order changed when writing names on cards and folders. Firm endings, such as Ltd., Inc., Co., Son, Bros., Mfg., and Corp., are treated as a unit in indexing and filing and are considered as though spelled in full, such as Brothers and Incorporated.

21. One or two words

Names that may be spelled either as one or two words are indexed and filed as one word.

22. Compound geographic names

Compound geographic names are considered as separate indexing and filing units, except when the first part of the name is not an English word, such as the Los in Los Angeles.

23. Titles or degrees of individuals, whether preceding or following the name, are not considered in indexing or filing. They are placed in parentheses after the given name or initial. Terms that designate seniority, such as Jr., Sr., 2d, are also placed in parentheses and are considered for indexing and filing only when the names to be indexed are otherwise identical.

Exception A:
When the name of an individual consists of a title and one name only, such as Queen Elizabeth, it is not transposed and the title is considered for indexing and filing.

Exception B:
When a title or foreign article is the initial word of a firm or association name, it is considered for indexing and filing.

24. Possessives

When a word ends in apostrophe s, the s is not considered in indexing and filing. However, when a word ends in s apostrophe, because the s is part of the original word, it is considered. This rule is sometimes stated, "Consider everything up to the apostrophe."

25. United States and foreign government names

Names pertaining to the federal government are indexed and filed under United States Government and then subdivided by title of the department, bureau, division, commission, or board. Names pertaining to foreign governments are indexed and filed under names of countries and then subdivided by title of the department, bureau, division, commission, or board. Phrases, such as department of, bureau of, division of, commission of, board of, when used in titles of governmental bodies, are placed in parentheses after the word they modify, but are disregarded in indexing and filing. Such phrases, however, are considered in indexing and filing nongovernmental names.

26. Other political subdivisions

Names pertaining to other political subdivisions, such as states, counties, cities, or towns, are indexed and filed under the name of the political subdivision and then subdivided by the title of the department, bureau, division, commission, or board.

27. Addresses

When the same name appears with different addresses, the names are indexed as usual and arranged alphabetically according to city or town. The State is considered only when there is duplication of both individual or company name and city name. If the same name is located at different addresses within the same city, then the names are arranged alphabetically by streets. If the same name is located at more than one address on the same street, then the names are arranged from the lower to the higher street number.

28. Numbers

Any number in a name is considered as though it were written in words, and it is indexed and filed as one unit.

29. Bank names

Because the names of many banking institutions are alike in several respects, as first National Bank, Second National Bank, etc., banks are indexed and filed first by city location, then by bank name, with the state location written in parentheses and considered only if necessary

30. Married women

The legal name of a married woman is the one used for filing purposes. Legally, a man's surname is the only part of a man's name a woman assumes when she marries. Her legal name, therefore, could be either:

   (1) Her own first and middle names together with her husband's surname, or
   (2) Her own first name and maiden surname, together with her husband's surname.

Mrs. is placed in parentheses at the end of the name. Her husband's first and middle names are given in parentheses below her legal name.

31. An alphabetically arranged list of names illustrating many difficult points of alphabetizing follows.

COLUMN I	COLUMN II
Abbott, W.B.	54th St. Tailor Shop
Abbott, Alice	Forstall, W.J.
Allen, Alexander B.	44th St. Garage
Allen, Alexander B., Inc.	M A Delivery Co.
Andersen, Hans	M & C Amusement Corp.
Andersen, Hans E.	M C Art Assn.
Andersen, Hans E., Jr.	MacAdam, Wm.
Anderson, Andrew	Macaulay, James
Andrews, George	MacAulay, Wilson
Brown Motor Co., Boston	MacDonald, R.J.
Brown Motor Co., Chicago	Macdonald, S.B.
Brown Motor Co., Philadelphia	Mace, Wm.
Brown Motor Co., San Francisco	MacMahon, L.S.
Dean, Anna	Madison, Seth
Dean, Anna F.	Mazza, Anthony
Dean, Anna Frances	McAdam, Wm.
Dean & Co.	McAndrews, Jerry
Deane-Arnold Apartments	Meade & Clark Co.
Deane's Pharmacy	Meade, S.T.
Deans, Felix A.	Meade, Solomon
Dean's Studio	Sackett Publishing Co.
Deans, Wm.	Sacks, Robert
Deans & Williams	St. Andrew Hotel
East Randolph	St. John, Homer W.
East St. Louis	Saks, Isaac B.
Easton, Pa.	Stephens, Ira
Eastport, Me.	Stevens, Delevan
	Stevens, Delila

IV. OFFICIAL EXAMINATION DIRECTIONS AND RULES

To preclude the possibility of conflicting or varying methods of filing, explicit directions and express rules are given to the candidate before he answers the filing questions on an examination.

The most recent official directions and rules for the filing questions are given immediately hereafter.

OFFICIAL DIRECTIONS

Each of questions ... to ... consists of four(five)names. For each question, select the one of the four(five)names that should be first (second)(third)(last) if the four(five)names were arranged in alphabetical order in accordance with the rules for alphabetical filing given below. Read these rules carefully. Then, for each question, indicate in the correspondingly numbered row on the answer sheet the letter preceding the name that should be first(second)(third)(last) in alphabetical order.

OFFICIAL RULES FOR ALPHABETICAL FILING

Names of Individuals

1. The names of individuals are filed in strict alphabetical order, first according to the last name, then according to first name or initial, and, finally, according to middle name or initial. For example: William Jones precedes George Kirk and Arthur S. Blake precedes Charles M. Blake.
2. When the last names are identical, the one with an initial instead of a first name precedes the one with a first name beginning with the same initial. For example: J. Green precedes Joseph Green.
3. When identical last names also have identical first names, the one without a middle name or initial precedes the one with a middle name or initial. For example: Robert Jackson precedes both Robert C. Jackson and Robert Chester Jackson.
4. When last names are identical and the first names are also identical, the one with a middle initial precedes the one with a middle name beginning with the same initial. For example: Peter A. Brown precedes Peter Alvin Brown.
5. Prefixes such as De, El, La, and Van are considered parts of the names they precede. For example: Wilfred DeWald precedes Alexander Duval.
6. Last names beginning with "Mac" or "Mc" are filed as spelled.
7. Abbreviated names are treated as if they were spelled out. For example: Jos. is filed as Joseph and Robt. is filed as Robert.
8. Titles and designations such as Dr., Mrs., Prof. are disregarded in filing.

Names of Business Organizations

1. The names of business organizations are filed exactly as written except that an organization bearing the name of an individual is filed alphabetically according to the name of the individual in accordance with the rules for filing names of individuals given above. For example: Thomas Allison Machine Company precedes Northern Baking Company.
2. When numerals occur in a name, they are treated as if they were spelled out. For example: 6 stands for six and 4th stands for fourth.
3. When the following words occur in names, they are disregarded: the, of, and. Sample: Choose the name that should be filed *third*.

    (A) Fred Town (2)   (C) D. Town   (1)
    (B) Jack Towne (3)   (D) Jack S. Towne (4)

The numbers in parentheses indicate the proper alphabetical order in which these names should be filed. Since the name that should be filed <u>third</u> is Jack Towne, the answer is (B).

EXAMINATION SECTION
TEST 1

DIRECTIONS: Questions 1 through 8 each show in Column I names written on four cards (lettered w, x, y, z) which have to be filed. You are to choose the option (lettered A, B, C, or D) in Column II which *BEST* represents the proper order of filing according to the Rules for Alphabetic Filing, given before, and the sample question given below. Print the letter of the correct answer in the space at the right.

SAMPLE QUESTION

Column I	Column II
w. Jane Earl	A. w, y, z, x
x. James A. Earle	B. y, w, z, x
y. James Earl	C. x, y, w, z
z. J. Earle	D. x, w, y, z

The correct way to file the cards is:
    y. James Earl
    w. Jane Earl
    z. J. Earle
    x. James A. Earle

The correct filing order is shown by the letters, y, w, z, x (in that sequence). Since, in Column II, B appears in front of the letters, y, w, z, x (in that sequence), B is the correct answer to the sample question.

Now answer the following questions using that same procedure.

Column I	Column II	
1. w. James Rothschild	A. x, z, w, y	1. ...
x. Julius B. Rothchild	B. x, w, z, y	
y. B. Rothstein	C. z, y, w, x	
z. Brian Joel Rothenstein	D. z, w, x, y	
2. w. George S. Wise	A. w, y, z, x	2. ...
x. S. G. Wise	B. x, w, y, z	
y. Geo. Stuart Wise	C. y, x, w, z	
z. Prof. Diana Wise	D. z, w, y, x	
3. w. 10th Street Bus Terminal	A. x, z, w, y	3. ...
x. Buckingham Travel Agency	B. y, x, w, z	
y. The Buckingham Theater	C. w, z, y, x	
z. Burt Tompkins Studio	D. x, w, y, z	
4. w. National Council of American Importers	A. w, y, x, z	4. ...
x. National Chain Co. of Providence	B. x, z, w, y	
y. National Council on Alcoholism	C. z, x, w, y	
z. National Chain Co.	D. z, x, y, w	
5. w. Dr. Herbert Alvary	A. w, y, x, z	5. ...
x. Mr. Victor Alvarado	B. z, w, x, y	
y. Alvar Industries	C. y, z, x, w	
z. V. Alvarado	D. w, z, x, y	
6. w. Joan MacBride	A. w, x, z, y	6. ...
x. Wm. Mackey	B. w, y, z, x	
y. Roslyn McKenzie	C. w, z, x, y	
z. Winifred Mackey	D. w, y, x, z	

	Column I	Column II	
7.	w. 3 Way Trucking Co.	A. y, x, z, w	7. ...
	x. 3rd Street Bakery	B. y, z, w, x	
	y. 380 Realty Corp.	C. x, y, z, w	
	z. Three Lions Pub	D. x, y, w, z	
8.	w. Miss Rose Leonard	A. z, w, x, y	8. ...
	x. Rev. Leonard Lucas	B. w, z, y, x	
	y. Sylvia Leonard Linen Shop	C. w, x, z, y	
	z. Rose S. Leonard	D. z, w, y, x	

TEST 2

DIRECTIONS: Questions 1 through 7 each show in Column I four names (lettered w, x, y, z) which have to be entered in an agency telephone directory. You are to choose the option (lettered A, B, C, or D) in Column II which *BEST* represents the proper order for entering them according to the Rules for Alphabetic Filing, given before, and the sample question given below.

SAMPLE QUESTION

	Column I	Column II
w.	Doris Jenkin	A. w, y, z, x
x.	Donald F. Jenkins	B. y, w, z, x
y.	Donald Jenkin	C. x, y, w, z
z.	D. Jenkins	D. x, w, y, z

The correct way to enter these names is:

y. Donald Jenkin
w. Doris Jenkin
z. D. Jenkins
x. Donald F. Jenkins

The correct order is shown by the letters y, w, z, x, in that sequence. Since, in Column II, B appears in front of the letters y, w, z, x, in that sequence, B is the correct answer to the sample question.

Now answer the following questions using the same procedure.

	Column I	Column II	
1.	w. Lawrence Robertson	A. x, y, w, z	1. ...
	x. Jack L. Robinson	B. w, z, x, y	
	y. John Robinson	C. z, w, x, y	
	z. William B. Roberson	D. z, w, y, x	
2.	w. P. N. Figueredo	A. y, x, z, w	2. ...
	x. M. Alice Figueroa	B. x, z, w, y	
	y. Jose Figueredo	C. x, w, z, y	
	z. M. Alicia Figueroa	D. y, w, x, z	
3.	w. George Steven Keats	A. y, x, w, z	3. ...
	x. George S. Keats	B. z, y, x, w	
	y. G. Samuel Keats	C. x, z, w, y	
	z. Dr. Samuel Keats	D. w, z, x, y	
4.	w. V. Merchant	A. w, x, y, z	4. ...
	x. Dr. William Mercher	B. w, y, z, x	
	y. Prof. Victor Merchant	C. z, y, w, x	
	z. Dr. Walter Merchan	D. z, w, y, x	

2

Column I	Column II	
5. w. Brian McCoy	A. z, x, y, w	5. ...
x. William Coyne	B. y, w, z, x	
y. Mr. William MacCoyle	C. x, z, y, w	
z. Dr. D. V. Coyne	D. w, y, z, x	
6. w. Ms. M. Rosie Buchanan	A. z, y, x, w	6. ...
x. Rosalyn M. Buchanan	B. w, z, x, y	
y. Rosie Maria Buchanan	C. w, z, y, x	
z. Rosa Marie Buchanan	D. z, x, y, w	
7. w. Prof. Jonathan Praga	A. w, z, y, x	7. ...
x. Dr. Joan Prager	B. w, x, z, y	
y. Alan VanPrague	C. x, w, z, y	
z. Alexander Prague	D. x, w, y, z	

TEST 3

DIRECTIONS: Questions 1 through 10 each show in Column I names written on four cards (lettered w, x, y, z) which have to be filed. You are to choose the option (lettered A, B, C, or D) in Column II which *BEST* represents the proper order of filing according to the rules and sample question given below. The cards are to be filed according to the Rules for Alphabetical Filing, given before, and the sample question given below.

SAMPLE QUESTION

Column I	Column II
w. Jane Earl	A. w, y, z, x
x. James A. Earle	B. y, w, z, x
y. James Earl	C. x, y, w, z
z. J. Earle	D. x, w, y, z

The correct way to file the cards is:
    y. James Earl
    w. Jane Earl
    z. J. Earle
    x. James A. Earle

The correct filing order is shown by the letters y, w, z, x (in that order). Since, in Column II, B appears in front of the letters y, w, z, x (in that order), B is the correct answer to the sample question.

Now answer Questions 1 through 10 using the same procedure.

Column I	Column II	
1. w. John Smith	A. w, x, y, z	1. ...
x. Joan Smythe	B. y, z, x, w	
y. Gerald Schmidt	C. y, z, w, x	
z. Gary Schmitt	D. z, y, w, x	
2. w. A. Black	A. w, x, y, z	2. ...
x. Alan S. Black	B. w, y, x, z	
y. Allan Black	C. w, y, z, x	
z. Allen A. Black	D. x, w, y, z	
3. w. Samuel Haynes	A. w, x, y, z	3. ...
x. Sam C. Haynes	B. x, w, z, y	
y. David Haynes	C. y, z, w, x	
z. Dave L. Haynes	D. z, y, x, w	

Column I	Column II	
4. w. Lisa B. McNeil x. Tom MacNeal y. Lisa McNeil z. Lorainne McNeal	A. x, y, w, z B. x, z, y, w C. y, w, z, x D. z, x, y, w	4. ...
5. w. Larry Richardson x. Leroy Richards y. Larry S. Richards z. Leroy C. Richards	A. w, y, x, z B. y, x, z, w C. y, z, x, w D. x, w, z, y	5. ...
6. w. Arlene Lane x. Arlene Cora Lane y. Arlene Clair Lane z. Arlene C. Lane	A. w, z, y, x B. w, z, x, y C. y, x, z, w D. z, y, w, x	
7. w. Betty Fish x. Prof. Ann Fish y. Norma Fisch z. Dr. Richard Fisch	A. w, x, z, y B. x, w, y, z C. y, z, x, w D. z, y, w, x	7. ...
8. w. Dr. Anthony David Lukak x. Mr. Steven Charles Lucas y. Mr. Anthony J. Lukak z. Prof. Steven C. Lucas	A. w, y, z, x B. x, z, w, y C. z, x, y, w D. z, x, w, y	8. ...
9. w. Martha Y. Lind x. Mary Beth Linden y. Martha W. Lind z. Mary Bertha Linden	A. w, y, z, x B. w, y, x, z C. y, w, z, x D. y, w, x, z	9. ...
10. w. Prof. Harry Michael MacPhelps x. Mr. Horace M. MacPherson y. Mr. Harold M. McPhelps z. Prof. Henry Martin MacPherson	A. w, z, x, y B. w, y, z, x C. z, x, w, y D. x, z, y, w	10. ...

TEST 4

DIRECTIONS: Answer Questions 1 through 5 on the basis of the following information:

A certain shop keeps an informational card file on all suppliers and merchandise. On each card is the supplier's name, the contract number for the merchandise he supplies, and a delivery date for the merchandise. In this filing system, the supplier's name is filed alphabetically, the contract number for the merchandise is filed numerically, and the delivery date is filed chronologically.

In Questions 1 through 5 there are five notations numbered 1 through 5 shown in Column I. Each notation is made up of a supplier's name, a contract number, and a date which is to be filed according to the following rules:

First: File in alphabetical order;
Second: When two or more notations have the same supplier, file according to the contract number in numerical order beginning with the lowest number;
Third: When two or more notations have the same supplier and contract number, file according to the date beginning with the earliest date.

In Column II the numbers 1 through 5 are arranged in four ways to show four different orders in which the merchandise information might

4

be filed. Pick the answer (A, B, C, or D) in Column II in which the notations are arranged according to the above filing rules.

SAMPLE QUESTION

Column I
1. Cluney (4865) 6/17/72
2. Roster (2466) 5/10/71
3. Altool (7114) 10/15/72
4. Cluney (5296) 12/18/71
5. Cluney (4865) 4/8/72

Column II
A. 2, 3, 4, 1, 5
B. 2, 5, 1, 3, 4
C. 3, 2, 1, 4, 5
D. 3, 5, 1, 4, 2

The correct way to file the cards is:
3. Altool (7114) 10/15/72
5. Cluney (4865) 4/8/72
1. Cluney (4865) 6/17/72
4. Cluney (5276) 12/18/71
2. Roster (2466) 5/10/71

Since the correct filing order is 3, 5, 1, 4, 2, the answer to the sample question is D. Now answer Questions 1 through 5.

	Column I		
1.	1. Warren	(96063)	3/30/73
	2. Moore	(21237)	9/4/74
	3. Newman	(10050)	12/12/73
	4. Downs	(81251)	1/2/73
	5. Oliver	(60145)	6/30/74
2.	1. Henry	(40552)	7/6/74
	2. Boyd	(91251)	9/1/73
	3. George	(8196)	12/12/73
	4. George	(31096)	1/12/74
	5. West	(6109)	8/9/73
3.	1. Salba	(4670)	9/7/73
	2. Salba	(51219)	3/1/73
	3. Crete	(81562)	7/1/74
	4. Salba	(51219)	1/11/74
	5. Texi	(31549)	1/25/73
4.	1. Crayone	(87105)	6/10/74
	2. Shamba	(49210)	1/5/73
	3. Valiant	(3152)	5/1/74
	4. Valiant	(3152)	1/9/74
	5. Poro	(59613)	7/1/73
5.	1. Mackie	(42169)	12/20/73
	2. Lebo	(5198)	9/12/72
	3. Drummon	(99631)	9/9/74
	4. Lebo	(15311)	1/25/72
	5. Harvin	(81765)	6/2/73

Column II

1.
A. 2, 4, 3, 5, 1
B. 2, 3, 5, 4, 1
C. 4, 5, 2, 3, 1
D. 4, 2, 3, 5, 1   1. ...

2.
A. 5, 4, 3, 1, 2
B. 2, 3, 4, 1, 5
C. 2, 4, 3, 1, 5
D. 5, 2, 3, 1, 4   2. ...

3.
A. 5, 3, 1, 2, 4
B. 3, 1, 2, 4, 5
C. 3, 5, 4, 2, 1
D. 5, 3, 4, 2, 1   3. ...

4.
A. 1, 2, 5, 3, 4
B. 1, 5, 2, 3, 4
C. 1, 5, 3, 4, 2
D. 1, 5, 2, 4, 3   4. ...

5.
A. 3, 2, 1, 5, 4
B. 3, 2, 4, 5, 1
C. 3, 5, 2, 4, 1
D. 3, 5, 4, 2, 1   5. ...

TEST 5

DIRECTIONS: Each of Questions 1 through 8 represents five cards to be filed, numbered 1 through 5 in Column I. Each card is made up of the employee's name, the date of a work assignment, and the work assignment code number shown in parentheses. The cards are to be filed according to the following rules:

First: File in alphabetical order;
Second: When two or more cards have the same employee's name,
         file according to the assignment date beginning with
         the earliest date;
Third: When two or more cards have the same employee's name
         and the same date, file according to the work assign-
         ment number beginning with the lowest number.

Column II shows the cards arranged in four different orders. Pick
the answer (A, B, C, or D) in Column II which shows the cards arranged correctly according to the above filing rules.

SAMPLE QUESTION

Column I			Column II
1. Cluney	4/8/72	(486503)	A. 2, 3, 4, 1, 5
2. Roster	5/10/71	(246611)	B. 2, 5, 1, 3, 4
3. Altool	10/15/72	(711433)	C. 3, 2, 1, 4, 5
4. Cluney	12/18/72	(527610)	D. 3, 5, 1, 4, 2
5. Cluney	4/8/72	(486500)	

The correct way to file the cards is:

3. Altool	10/15/72	(711433)
5. Cluney	4/8/72	(486500)
1. Cluney	4/8/72	(486503)
4. Cluney	12/18/72	(527610)
2. Roster	5/10/71	(246611)

The correct filing order is shown by the numbers in front of each
name (3, 5, 1, 4, 2). The answer to the sample question is the letter
in Column II in front of the numbers 3, 5, 1, 4, 2. This answer is D.

Now answer Questions 1 through 8 according to these rules.

	Column I			Column II	
1.	1. Kohls	4/2/72	(125677)	A. 1, 2, 3, 4, 5	1. ...
	2. Keller	3/21/72	(129698)	B. 3, 2, 1, 4, 5	
	3. Jackson	4/10/72	(213541)	C. 3, 1, 2, 4, 5	
	4. Richards	1/9/73	(347236)	D. 5, 2, 1, 3, 4	
	5. Richmond	12/11/71	(379321)		
2.	1. Burroughs	5/27/72	(237896)	A. 1, 4, 3, 2, 5	2. ...
	2. Charlson	1/16/72	(114537)	B. 4, 1, 5, 3, 2	
	3. Carlsen	12/2/72	(114377)	C. 1, 4, 3, 5, 2	
	4. Burton	5/1/72	(227096)	D. 4, 1, 3, 5, 2	
	5. Charlson	12/2/72	(114357)		
3.	1. Ungerer	11/11/72	(537924)	A. 1, 5, 3, 2, 4	3. ...
	2. Winters	11/10/72	(657834)	B. 5, 1, 3, 4, 2	
	3. Ventura	12/1/72	(698694)	C. 3, 5, 1, 2, 4	
	4. Winters	10/11/72	(675654)	D. 1, 5, 3, 4, 2	
	5. Ungaro	11/10/72	(684325)		
4.	1. Norton	3/12/73	(071605)	A. 1, 4, 2, 3, 5	4. ...
	2. Morris	2/26/73	(068931)	B. 3, 5, 2, 4, 1	
	3. Morse	5/12/73	(142358)	C. 2, 4, 3, 5, 1	
	4. Morris	2/26/73	(068391)	D. 4, 2, 5, 3, 1	
	5. Morse	2/26/73	(068391)		
5.	1. Eger	4/19/72	(874129)	A. 3, 4, 1, 2, 5	5. ...
	2. Eihler	5/19/73	(875329)	B. 1, 4, 5, 2, 3	
	3. Ehrlich	11/19/72	(874839)	C. 4, 1, 3, 2, 5	
	4. Eger	4/19/72	(876129)	D. 1, 4, 3, 5, 2	
	5. Eihler	5/19/72	(874239)		

		Column I			Column II						
6.	1. Johnson	12/21/72	(786814)	A.	2, 4, 3, 5, 1						6. ...
	2. Johns	12/21/73	(801024)	B.	4, 2, 5, 3, 1						
	3. Johnson	12/12/73	(762814)	C.	4, 5, 3, 1, 2						
	4. Jackson	12/12/73	(862934)	D.	5, 3, 1, 2, 4						
	5. Johnson	12/12/73	(762184)								
7.	1. Fuller	7/12/72	(598310)	A.	2, 1, 5, 4, 3						7. ...
	2. Fuller	7/2/72	(598301)	B.	1, 2, 4, 5, 3						
	3. Fuller	7/22/72	(598410)	C.	1, 4, 5, 2, 3						
	4. Fuller	7/17/73	(598710)	D.	2, 1, 3, 5, 4						
	5. Fuller	7/17/73	(598701)								
8.	1. Perrine	10/27/69	(637096)	A.	3, 4, 5, 1, 2						8. ...
	2. Perrone	11/14/72	(767609)	B.	3, 2, 5, 4, 1						
	3. Perrault	10/15/68	(629706)	C.	5, 3, 4, 1, 2						
	4. Perrine	10/17/72	(373656)	D.	4, 5, 1, 2, 3						
	5. Perine	10/17/71	(376356)								

TEST 6

DIRECTIONS FOR THIS SECTION:

Each question or incomplete statement is followed by several suggested answers or completions. Select the one that *BEST* answers the question or completes the statement. *PRINT THE LETTER OF THE CORRECT ANSWER IN THE SPACE AT THE RIGHT.*

1. *Which one* of the following *BEST* describes the usual arrangement of a tickler file?   1. ...
   A. Alphabetical   B. Chronological
   C. Numerical   D. Geographical

2. *Which one* of the following is the *LEAST* desirable filing practice?   2. ...
   A. Using staples to keep papers together
   B. Filing all material without regard to date
   C. Keeping a record of all materials removed from the files
   D. Writing filing instructions on each paper prior to filing

3. The *one* of the following records which it would be *MOST* advisable to keep in alphabetical order is a   3. ...
   A. continuous listing of phone messages, including time and caller, for your supervisor
   B. listing of individuals currently employed by your agency in a particular title
   C. record of purchases paid for by the petty cash fund
   D. dated record of employees who have borrowed material from the files in your office

4. Tickler systems are used in many legal offices for scheduling and calendar control. Of the following, the *LEAST* common use of a tickler system is to   4. ...
   A. keep papers filed in such a way that they may easily be retrieved
   B. arrange for the appearance of witnesses when they will be needed

7

C. remind lawyers when certain papers are due
D. arrange for the gathering of certain types of evidence
5. A type of file which permits the operator to remain   5. ...
   seated while the file can be moved backward and forward
   as required is *BEST* termed a
     A. lateral file   B. movable file
     C. reciprocating file   D. rotary file
6. In which of the following cases would it be *MOST* desirable   6. ...
   to have two cards for one individual in a single alphabetic file? The individual has
     A. a hyphenated surname   B. two middle names
     C. a first name with an unusual spelling
     D. a compound first name

KEY (CORRECT ANSWERS)

TEST 1	TEST 2	TEST 3
1. A	1. C	1. C
2. D	2. D	2. A
3. B	3. A	3. D
4. D	4. D	4. B
5. C	5. A	5. B
6. A	6. B	6. A
7. C	7. B	7. C
8. B		8. D
		9. C
		10. A

TEST 4	TEST 5	TEST 6
1. D	1. B	1. B
2. B	2. A	2. B
3. B	3. B	3. B
4. D	4. D	4. A
5. C	5. D	5. C
	6. B	6. A
	7. D	
	8. C	

CODING
EXAMINATION SECTION

Commentary/Test 1

COMMENTARY

An ingenious question-type called coding, involving elements of alphabetizing, filing, name and number comparison, and evaluative judgment and application, has currently won wide acceptance in testing circles for measuring clerical aptitude and general ability, particularly on the senior (middle) grades (levels).

While the directions for this question usually vary in detail, the candidate is generally asked to consider groups of names, codes, and numbers, and, then, according to a given plan, to arrange codes in alphabetic order; to arrange these in numerical sequence; to re-arrange columns of names and numbers in correct order; to espy errors in coding; to choose the correct coding arrangement in consonance with the given directions and examples, etc.

This question-type appears to have few parameters in respect to form, substance, or degree of difficulty.

Accordingly, acquaintance with, and practice in, the coding question is recommended for the serious candidate.

EXAMINATION SECTION

TEST 1

DIRECTIONS FOR THIS SECTION: Questions 1 through 10 are to be answered on the basis of the following Code Table. In this table every letter has a corresponding code number to be punched. Each question contains three lines of letters and code numbers. In each line, the code numbers should correspond with the letters in accordance with the table.

Letter	M	X	R	T	W	A	E	Q	Z	C
Code	1	2	3	4	5	6	7	8	9	0

On some of the lines, an error exists in the coding. Compare the letters and numbers in each question carefully. If you find an error or errors on

    only *one* of the lines in the question, mark your answer A;
    any *two* lines in the question, mark your answer B;
    all *three* lines in the question, mark your answer C;
    none of the lines in the question, mark your answer D.

SAMPLE QUESTION

XAQMZMRQ	–	26819138
RAERQEX	–	3573872
TMZCMTZA	–	46901496

In the above sample, the first line is correct since each letter, as listed, has the correct corresponding code number.

In the second line, an error exists because the letter A should have the code number 6 instead of 5.

In the third line, an error exists because the letter W should have the code number 5 instead of 6.

Since there are errors in two of the three lines, your answer should be B.

1

1.	EQRMATTR	–	78316443	1. ...
	MACWXRQW	–	16052385	
	XZEMCAR	–	2971063	
2.	CZEMRXQ	–	0971238	2. ...
	XMTARET	–	2146374	
	WCEARWEC	–	50863570	
3.	CEXAWRQZ	–	07265389	3. ...
	RCRMMZQT	–	33011984	
	ACMZWTEX	–	60195472	
4.	XRCZQZWR	–	23089953	4. ...
	CMRQCAET	–	01389574	
	ZXRWTECM	–	92345701	
5.	AXMTRAWR	–	62134653	5. ...
	EQQCZCEW	–	77809075	
	MAZQARTM	–	16086341	
6.	WRWQCTRM	–	53580431	6. ...
	CXMWAERZ	–	02156739	
	RCQEWWME	–	30865517	
7.	CRMECEAX	–	03170762	7. ...
	MZCTRXRQ	–	19043238	
	XXZREMEW	–	22937175	
8.	MRCXQEAX	–	13928762	8. ...
	WAMZTRMZ	–	65194319	
	ECXARWXC	–	70263520	
9.	MAWXECRQ	–	16527038	9. ...
	RXQEAETM	–	32876741	
	RXEWMCZQ	–	32751098	
10.	MRQZCATE	–	13890647	10. ...
	WCETRXAW	–	50743625	
	CZWMCERT	–	09510734	

TEST 2

DIRECTIONS FOR THIS SECTION: Questions 1 through 6 consist of three
lines of code letters and numbers. The numbers on each line should
correspond with the code letters on the same line in accordance with
the table below.

Code Letter	F	X	L	M	R	W	T	S	B	H
Corresponding Number	0	1	2	3	4	5	6	7	8	9

On some of the lines, an error exists in the coding. Compare the
letters and numbers in each question carefully. If you find an error
or errors on
        only *one* of the lines in the question, mark your answer A;
        any *two* lines in the question, mark your answer B;
        all *three* lines in the question, mark your answer C;
        none of the lines in the question, mark your answer D.

2

SAMPLE QUESTION

```
LTSXHMF 2671930
TBRWHLM 6845913
SXLBFMR 5128034
```

In the above sample, the first line is correct since each code letter listed has the correct corresponding number.

On the second line, an error exists because code letter L should have the number 2 instead of the number 1.

On the third line, an error exists because the code letter S should have the number 7 instead of the number 5.

Since there are errors on two of the three lines, the correct answer is B.

1. XMWBHLR   1358924   1. ...
   FWSLRHX   0572491
   MTXBLTS   3618267
2. XTLSMRF   1627340   2. ...
   BMHRFLT   8394026
   HLTSWRX   9267451
3. LMBSFXS   2387016   3. ...
   RWLMBSX   4532871
   SMFXBHW   7301894
4. RSTWTSML   47657632   4. ...
   LXRMHFBS   21439087
   FTLBMRWX   06273451
5. XSRSBWFM   17478603   5. ...
   BRMXRMXT   84314216
   XSTFBWRL   17609542
6. TMSBXHLS   63781927   6. ...
   RBSFLFWM   48702053
   MHFXWTRS   39015647

TEST 3

DIRECTIONS FOR THIS SECTION: Questions 1 through 5 consist of three lines of code letters and numbers. The numbers on each line should correspond with the code letters on the same line in accordance with the table below.

Code Letter	P	L	I	J	B	O	H	U	C	G
Corresponding Number	0	1	2	3	4	5	6	7	8	9

On some of the lines, an error exists in the coding. Compare the letters and numbers in each question carefully. If you find an error or errors on

    only *one* of the lines in the question, mark your answer A;
    any *two* lines in the question, mark your answer B;
    all *three* lines in the question, mark your answer C;
    none of the lines in the question, mark your answer D.

JHOILCP	3652180
BICLGUP	4286970
UCIBHLJ	5824613

In the above sample, the first line is correct since each code letter listed has the correct corresponding number.

On the second line, an error exists because code letter L should have the number 1 instead of the number 6.

On the third line an error exists because the code letter U should have the number 7 instead of the number 5.

Since there are errors on two of the three lines, the correct answer is B.

1. BULJCIP 4713920   1. ...
   HIGPOUL 6290571
   OCUHJBI 5876342
2. CUBLOIJ 8741023   2. ...
   LCLGCLB 1818914
   JPUHIOC 3076158
3. OIJGCBPO 52398405   3. ...
   UHPBLIOP 76041250
   CLUIPGPC 81720908
4. BPCOUOJI 40875732   4. ...
   UOHCIPLB 75682014
   GLHUUCBJ 92677843
5. HOIOHJLH 65256361   5. ...
   IOJJHHBP 25536640
   OJHBJOPI 53642502

TEST 4

DIRECTIONS FOR THIS SECTION: Questions 1 through 5 consist of three lines of code letters and numbers. The numbers on each line should correspond with the code letters on the same line in accordance with the table below.

Code Letters	Q	S	L	Y	M	O	U	N	W	Z
Corresponding Numbers	1	2	3	4	5	6	7	8	9	0

On some of the lines, an error exists in the coding. Compare the letters and numbers in each question carefully. If you find an error on

only *one* of the lines in the question, mark your answer A;
any *two* lines in the question, mark your answer B;
all *three* lines in the question, mark your answer C;
none of the lines in the question, mark your answer D.

SAMPLE QUESTION

MOQNWZQS	56189012
QWNMOLYU	19865347
LONLMYWN	36835489

4

In the above sample, the first line is correct since each code letter, as listed, has the correct corresponding number.

On the second line, an error exists because code letter M should have the number 5 instead of the number 6.

On the third line an error exists because the code letter W should have the number 9 instead of the number 8.

Since there are errors on two of the three lines, the correct answer is B.

1. SMUWOLQN   25796318   1. ...
   ULSQNMZL   73218503
   NMYQZUSL   85410723
2. YUWWMYQZ   47995410   2. ...
   SOSOSQSO   26262126
   ZUNLWMYW   07839549
3. QULSWZYN   17329045   3. ...
   ZYLQWOYW   04319639
   QLUYWZSO   13749026   .
4. NLQZOYUM   83106475   4. ...
   SQMUWZOM   21579065
   MMYWMZSQ   55498021
5. NQLOWZZU   81319007   5. ...
   SMYLUNZO   25347806
   UWMSNZOL   79528013

TEST 5

DIRECTIONS FOR THIS SECTION: Answer Questions 1 through 6 *SOLELY* on the basis of the chart and the instructions given below.

Toll Rate	$.25	$.30	$.45	$.60	$.75	$.90	$1.20	$2.50
Classification Number of Vehicle	1	2	3	4	5	6	7	8

Assume that each of the amounts of money on the above chart is a toll rate charged for a type of vehicle and that the number immediately below each amount is the classification number for that type of vehicle. For instance, "1" is the classification number for a vehicle paying a $.25 toll; "2" is the classification number for a vehicle paying a $.30 toll; and so forth.

In each question, a series of tolls is given in Column I. Column II gives four different arrangements of classification numbers. You are to pick the answer (A, B, C, or D) in Column II that gives the classification numbers that match the tolls in Column I and are in the same order as the tolls in Column I.

SAMPLE QUESTION

Column I   Column II
$.30, $.90, $2.50, $.45   A. 2, 6, 8, 2
                                 B. 2, 8, 6, 3
                                 C. 2, 6, 8, 3
                                 D. 1, 6, 8, 3

According to the chart, the classification numbers that correspond to these toll rates are as follows: $.30 - 2, $.90 - 6, $2.50 - 8, $.45 - 3. Therefore, the right answer is 2, 6, 8, 3. The answer is C in Column II.

Do the following questions in the same way.

<u>Column I</u>

<u>Column II</u>

1. $.60, $.30, $.90, $1.20, $.60
   A. 4, 6, 2, 8, 4
   B. 4, 2, 6, 7, 4
   C. 2, 4, 7, 6, 2
   D. 2, 4, 6, 7, 4

1. ...

2. $.90, $.45, $.25, $.45, $2.50, $.75
   A. 6, 3, 1, 3, 8, 3
   B. 6, 3, 3, 1, 8, 5
   C. 6, 1, 3, 3, 8, 5
   D. 6, 3, 1, 3, 8, 5

2. ...

3. $.45, $.75, $1.20, $.25, $.25, $.30, $.45
   A. 3, 5, 7, 1, 1, 2, 3
   B. 5, 3, 7, 1, 1, 2, 3
   C. 3, 5, 7, 1, 2, 1, 3
   D. 3, 7, 5, 1, 1, 2, 3

3. ...

4. $1.20, $2.50, $.45, $.90, $1.20, $.75, $.25
   A. 7, 8, 5, 6, 7, 5, 1
   B. 7, 8, 3, 7, 6, 5, 1
   C. 7, 8, 3, 6, 7, 5, 1
   D. 7, 8, 3, 6, 7, 1, 5

4. ...

5. $2.50, $1.20, $.90, $.25, $.60, $.45, $.30
   A. 8, 6, 7, 1, 4, 3, 2
   B. 8, 7, 5, 1, 4, 3, 2
   C. 8, 7, 6, 2, 4, 3, 2
   D. 8, 7, 6, 1, 4, 3, 2

5. ...

6. $.75, $.25, $.45, $.60, $.90, $.30, $2.50
   A. 5, 1, 3, 2, 4, 6, 8
   B. 5, 1, 3, 4, 2, 6, 8
   C. 5, 1, 3, 4, 6, 2, 8
   D. 5, 3, 1, 4, 6, 2, 8

6. ...

TEST 6

DIRECTIONS FOR THIS SECTION: Answer Questions 1 through 10 on the basis of the following information:

A code number for any item is obtained by combining the date of delivery, number of units received, and number of units used.

The first two digits represent the day of the month, the third and fourth digits represent the month, and the fifth and sixth digits represent the year.

The number following the letter R represents the number of units received and the number following the letter U represents the number of units used.

For example, the code number 120673-R5690-U1001 indicates that a delivery of 5,690 units was made on June 12, 1973 of which 1,001 units were used.

Questions 1-6.
DIRECTIONS: Using the chart below, answer Questions 1 through 6 by choosing the letter (A, B, C, or D) in which the supplier and stock number correspond to the code number given.

Supplier	Stock Number	Number of Units Received	Delivery Date	Number of Units Used
Stony	38390	8300	May 11, 1972	3800
Stoney	39803	1780	September 15, 1973	1703
Nievo	21220	5527	October 10, 1973	5007
Nieve	38903	1733	August 5, 1973	1703
Monte	39213	5527	October 10, 1972	5007
Stony	38890	3308	December 9, 1972	3300
Stony	83930	3880	September 12, 1972	380
Nevo	47101	485	June 11, 1972	231
Nievo	12122	5725	May 11, 1973	5201
Neve	47101	9721	August 15, 1973	8207
Nievo	21120	2275	January 7, 1972	2175
Rosa	41210	3821	March 3, 1973	2710
Stony	38890	3308	September 12, 1972	3300
Dinal	54921	1711	April 2, 1973	1117
Stony	33890	8038	March 5, 1973	3300
Dinal	54721	1171	March 2, 1972	717
Claridge	81927	3308	April 5, 1973	3088
Nievo	21122	4878	June 7, 1972	3492
Haley	39670	8300	December 23, 1973	5300

1. Code No. 120972-R3308-U3300   1. ...
   A. Nievo - 12122   B. Stony - 83930
   C. Nievo - 21220   D. Stony - 38890
2. Code No. 101072-R5527-U5007   2. ...
   A. Nievo - 21220   B. Haley - 39670
   C. Monte - 39213   D. Claridge - 81927
3. Code No. 101073-R5527-U5007   3. ...
   A. Nievo - 21220   B. Monte - 39213
   C. Nievo - 12122   D. Nievo - 21120
4. Code No. 110573-R5725-U5201   4. ...
   A. Nievo - 12122   B. Nievo - 21220
   C. Haley - 39670   D. Stony - 38390
5. Code No. 070172-R2275-U2175   5. ...
   A. Stony - 33890   B. Stony - 83930
   C. Stony - 38390   D. Nievo - 21120
6. Code No. 120972-R3880-U380   6. ...
   A. Stony - 83930   B. Stony - 38890
   C. Stony - 33890   D. Monte - 39213

Questions 7-10.
DIRECTIONS: Using the same chart, answer Questions 7 through 10 by choosing the letter (A, B, C, or D) in which the code number corresponds to the supplier and stock number given.
7. Nieve - 38903   7. ...
   A. 851973-R1733-U1703   B. 080572-R1733-U1703
   C. 080573-R1733-U1703   D. 050873-R1733-U1703

8. Nevo - 47101
    A. 081573-R9721-U8207   B. 091573-R9721-U8207
    C. 110672-R485-U231   D. 061172-R485-U231
9. Dinal - 54921
    A. 020473-R1711-U1117   B. 030272-R1171-U717
    C. 020372-R1171-U717   D. 421973-R1711-U1117
10. Nievo - 21122
    A. 070672-R4878-U3492   B. 060772-R4878-U349
    C. 761972-R4878-U3492   D. 060772-R4878-U3492

8. ...

9. ...

10. ...

KEYS (CORRECT ANSWERS)

TEST 1	TEST 2	TEST 3
1. D	1. D	1. A
2. B	2. A	2. C
3. A	3. C	3. D
4. C	4. B	4. B
5. C	5. C	5. C
6. A	6. D	
7. D		
8. B		
9. D		
10. A		

TEST 4	TEST 5	TEST 6
1. D	1. B	1. D
2. D	2. D	2. C
3. B	3. A	3. A
4. A	4. C	4. A
5. C	5. D	5. D
	6. C	6. A
		7. D
		8. C
		9. A
		10. A

PHILOSOPHY, PRINCIPLES, PRACTICES, AND TECHNICS
OF
SUPERVISION, ADMINISTRATION, MANAGEMENT, AND ORGANIZATION

I. MEANING OF SUPERVISION

The extension of the democratic philosophy has been accompanied by an extension in the scope of supervision. Modern leaders and supervisors no longer think of supervision in the narrow sense of being confined chiefly to visiting employees, supplying materials, or rating the staff. They regard supervision as being intimately related to all the concerned agencies of society, they speak of the supervisor's function in terms of "growth", rather than the "improvement," of employees

This modern concept of supervision may be defined as follows:

Supervision is leadership and the development of leadership within groups which are cooperatively engaged in inspection, research, training, guidance and evaluation.

II. THE OLD AND THE NEW SUPERVISION

TRADITIONAL	*MODERN*
1. Inspection	1. Study and analysis
2. Focused on the employee	2. Focused on aims, materials, methods, supervisors, employees, environment
3. Visitation	3. Demonstrations, intervisitation, workshops, directed reading, bulletins, etc.
4. Random and haphazard	4. Definitely organized and planned (scientific)
5. Imposed and authoritarian	5. Cooperative and democratic
6. One person usually	6. Many persons involved (creative)

III. THE EIGHT (8) BASIC PRINCIPLES OF THE NEW SUPERVISION

1. *PRINCIPLE OF RESPONSIBILITY*

   Authority to act and responsibility for acting must be joined.
   a. If you give responsibility, give authority.
   b. Define employee duties clearly.
   c. Protect employees from criticism by others.
   d. Recognize the rights as well as obligations of employees.
   e. Achieve the aims of a democratic society insofar as it is possible within the area of your work.
   f. Establish a situation favorable to training and learning.
   g. Accept ultimate responsibility for everything done in your section, unit, office, division, department.
   h. Good administration and good supervision are inseparable.

2. *PRINCIPLE OF AUTHORITY*

   The success of the supervisor is measured by the extent to which the power of authority is not used.
   a. Exercise simplicity and informality in supervision.
   b. Use the simplest machinery of supervision.
   c. If it is good for the organization as a whole, it is probably justified.
   d. Seldom be arbitrary or authoritative.
   e. Do not base your work on the power of position or of personality.
   f. Permit and encourage the free expression of opinions.

3. *PRINCIPLE OF SELF-GROWTH*

   The success of the supervisor is measured by the extent to which, and the speed with which, he is no longer needed.
   a. Base criticism on principles, not on specifics.
   b. Point out higher activities to employees.

c. Train for self-thinking by employees, to meet new situations.
 d. Stimulate initiative, self-reliance and individual responsibility.
 e. Concentrate on stimulating the growth of employees rather than on removing defects.

4. *PRINCIPLE OF INDIVIDUAL WORTH*
 Respect for the individual is a paramount consideration in supervision.
 a. Be human and sympathetic in dealing with employees.
 b. Don't nag about things to be done.
 c. Recognize the individual differences among employees and seek opportunities to permit best expression of each personality.

5. *PRINCIPLE OF CREATIVE LEADERSHIP*
 The best supervision is that which is not apparent to the employee.
 a. Stimulate, don't drive employees to creative action.
 b. Emphasize doing good things.
 c. Encourage employees to do what they do best.
 d. Do not be too greatly concerned with details of subject or method.
 e. Do not be concerned exclusively with immediate problems and activities.
 f. Reveal higher activities and make them both desired and maximally possible.
 g. Determine procedures in the light of each situation but see that these are derived from a sound basic philosophy.
 h. Aid, inspire and lead so as to liberate the creative spirit latent in all good employees.

6. *PRINCIPLE OF SUCCESS AND FAILURE*
 There are no unsuccessful employees, only unsuccessful supervisors who have failed to give proper leadership.
 a. Adapt suggestions to the capacities, attitudes, and prejudices of employees.
 b. Be gradual, be progressive, be persistent.
 c. Help the employee find the general principle; have the employee apply his own problem to the general principle.
 d. Give adequate appreciation for good work and honest effort.
 e. Anticipate employee difficulties and help to prevent them.
 f. Encourage employees to do the desirable things they will do anyway.
 g. Judge your supervision by the results it secures.

7. *PRINCIPLE OF SCIENCE*
 Successful supervision is scientific, objective, and experimental. It is based on facts, not on prejudices.
 a. Be cumulative in results.
 b. Never divorce your suggestions from the goals of training.
 c. Don't be impatient of results.
 d. Keep all matters on a professional, not a personal level.
 e. Do not be concerned exclusively with immediate problems and activities.
 f. Use objective means of determining achievement and rating where possible.

8. *PRINCIPLE OF COOPERATION*
 Supervision is a cooperative enterprise between supervisor and employee.
 a. Begin with conditions as they are.
 b. Ask opinions of all involved when formulating policies.

          c. Organization is as good as its weakest link.
          d. Let employees help to determine policies and department
             programs.
          e. Be approachable and accessible - physically and mentally.
          f. Develop pleasant social relationships.
IV. WHAT IS ADMINISTRATION?
     Administration is concerned with providing the environment, the
material facilities,and the operational procedures that will promote
the maximum growth and development of supervisors and employees. (Organization is an aspect,and a concomitant,of administration.)
     There is no sharp line of demarcation between supervision and ad-
ministration; these functions are intimately interrelated and,often,
overlapping. They are complementary activities.
     1. *PRACTICES COMMONLY CLASSED AS "SUPERVISORY"*
          a. Conducting employees conferences
          b. Visiting sections,units,offices,divisions,departments
          c. Arranging for demonstrations
          d. Examining plans
          e. Suggesting professional reading
          f. Interpreting bulletins
          g. Recommending in-service training courses
          h. Encouraging experimentation
          i. Appraising employee morale
          j. Providing for intervisitation
     2. *PRACTICES COMMONLY CLASSIFIED AS "ADMINISTRATIVE"*
          a. Management of the office
          b. Arrangement of schedules for extra duties
          c. Assignment of rooms or areas
          d. Distribution of supplies
          e. Keeping records and reports
          f. Care of audio-visual materials
          g. Keeping inventory records
          h. Checking record cards and books
          i. Programming special activities
          j. Checking on the attendance and punctuality of employees
     3. *PRACTICES COMMONLY CLASSIFIED AS BOTH "SUPERVISORY" AND
        "ADMINISTRATIVE"*
          a. Program construction
          b. Testing or evaluating outcomes
          c. Personnel accounting
          d. Ordering instructional materials
V. RESPONSIBILITIES OF THE SUPERVISOR
     A person employed in a supervisory capacity must constantly be
able to improve his own efficiency and ability. He represents the
employer to the employees and only continuous self-examination can
make him a capable supervisor.
     Leadership and training are the supervisor's responsibility. An
efficient working unit is one in which the employees work with the
supervisor. It is his job to bring out the best in his employees.
He must always be relaxed,courteous and calm in his association with
his employees. Their feelings are important, and a harsh attitude
does not develop the most efficient employees.

VI. COMPETENCIES OF THE SUPERVISOR
   1. Complete knowledge of the duties and responsibilities of his position.
   2. To be able to organize a job, plan ahead and carry through.
   3. To have self-confidence and initiative.
   4. To be able to handle the unexpected situation and make quick decisions.
   5. To be able to properly train subordinates in the positions they are best suited for.
   6. To be able to keep good human relations among his subordinates.
   7. To be able to keep good human relations between his subordinates and himself and to earn their respect and trust.

VII. THE PROFESSIONAL SUPERVISOR-EMPLOYEE RELATIONSHIP

There are two kinds of efficiency: one kind is only apparent and is produced in organizations through the exercise of mere discipline; this is but a simulation of the second, or true, efficiency which springs from spontaneous cooperation. If you are a manager, no matter how great or small your responsibility, it is your job, in the final analysis, to create and develop this involuntary cooperation among the people whom you supervise. For, no matter how powerful a combination of money, machines, and materials a company may have, this is a dead and sterile thing without a team of willing, thinking and articulate people to guide it.

The following 21 points are presented as indicative of the exemplary basic relationship that should exist between supervisor and employee:
   1. Each person wants to be liked and respected by his fellow employee and wants to be treated with consideration and respect by his superior.
   2. The most competent employee will make an error. However, in a unit where good relations exist between the supervisor and his employees, tenseness and fear do not exist. Thus, errors are not hidden or covered up and the efficiency of a unit is not impaired.
   3. Subordinates resent rules, regulations, or orders that are unreasonable or unexplained.
   4. Subordinates are quick to resent unfairness, harshness, injustices and favoritism.
   5. An employee will accept responsibility if he knows that he will be complimented for a job well done, and not too harshly chastized for failure; that his supervisor will check the cause of the failure, and, if it was the supervisor's fault, he will assume the blame therefor. If it was the employee's fault, his supervisor will explain the correct method or means of handling the responsibility.
   6. An employee wants to receive credit for a suggestion he has made, that is used. If a suggestion cannot be used, the employee is entitled to an explanation. The supervisor should not say "no" and close the subject.
   7. Fear and worry slow up a worker's ability. Poor working environment can impair his physical and mental health. A good supervisor avoids forceful methods, threats and arguments to get a job done.
   8. A forceful supervisor is able to train his employees individually and as a team, and is able to motivate them in the proper channels.

4

9. A mature supervisor is able to properly evaluate his subordinates and to keep them happy and satisfied.
10. A sensitive supervisor will never patronize his subordinates.
11. A worthy supervisor will respect his employees' confidences.
12. Definite and clear-cut responsibilities should be assigned to each executive.
13. Responsibility should always be coupled with corresponding authority.
14. No change should be made in the scope or responsibilities of a position without a definite understanding to that effect on the part of all persons concerned.
15. No executive or employee,occupying a single position in the organization,should be subject to definite orders from more than one source.
16. Orders should never be given to subordinates over the head of a responsible executive. Rather than do this, the officer in question should be supplanted.
17. Criticisms of subordinates should,whever possible,be made privately, and in no case should a subordinate be criticized in the presence of executives or employees of equal or lower rank.
18. No dispute or difference between executives or employees as to authority or responsibilities should be considered too trivial for prompt and careful adjudication.
19. Promotions,wage changes,and disciplinary action should always be approved by the executive immediately superior to the one directly responsible.
20. No executive or employee should ever be required,or expected,to be at the same time an assistant to, and critic of, another.
21. Any executive whose work is subject to regular inspection should, whever practicable, be given the assistance and facilities necessary to enable him to maintain an independent check of the quality of his work.

VIII. MINI-TEXT IN SUPERVISION,ADMINISTRATION,MANAGEMENT,AND ORGANIZATION
A. BRIEF HIGHLIGHTS
Listed concisely and sequentially are major headings and important data in the field for quick recall and review.
1. *LEVELS OF MANAGEMENT*
Any organization of some size has several levels of management. In terms of a ladder the levels are:

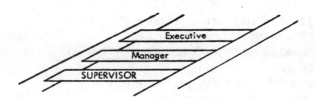

The first level is very important because it is the beginning point of management leadership.
2. *WHAT THE SUPERVISOR MUST LEARN*
A supervisor must learn to:
(1) Deal with people and their differences
(2) Get the job done through people
(3) Recognize the problems when they exist
(4) Overcome obstacles to good performance
(5) Evaluate the performance of people
(6) Check his own performance in terms of accomplishment

3. *A DEFINITION OF SUPERVISOR*

The term supervisor means any individual having authority, in the interests of the employer, to hire, transfer, suspend, lay-off, recall, promote, discharge, assign, reward, or discipline other employees... or responsibility to direct them, or to adjust their grievances, or effectively to recommend such action, if, in connection with the foregoing, exercise of such authority is not of a merely routine or clerical nature but requires the use of independent judgment.

4. *ELEMENTS OF THE TEAM CONCEPT*

What is involved in teamwork? The component parts are:

(1) Members   (3) Goals   (5) Cooperation
(2) A leader   (4) Plans   (6) Spirit

5. *PRINCIPLES OF ORGANIZATION*

(1) A team member must know what his job is
(2) Be sure that the nature and scope of a job are understood
(3) Authority and responsibility should be carefully spelled out
(4) A supervisor should be permitted to make the maximum number of decisions affecting his employees
(5) Employees should report to only one supervisor
(6) A supervisor should direct only as many employees as he can handle effectively
(7) An organization plan should be flexible
(8) Inspection and performance of work should be separate
(9) Organizational problems should receive immediate attention
(10) Assign work in line with ability and experience

6. *THE FOUR IMPORTANT PARTS OF EVERY JOB*

(1) Inherent in every job is the *accountability* for results
(2) A second set of factors in every job are *responsibilities*
(3) Along with duties and responsibilities one must have the *authority* to act within certain limits without obtaining permission to proceed
(4) No job exists in a vacuum. The supervisor is surrounded by key *relationships*

7. *PRINCIPLES OF DELEGATION*

Where work is delegated for the first time, the supervisor should think in terms of these questions:

(1) Who is best qualified to do this?
(2) Can an employee improve his abilities by doing this?
(3) How long should an employee spend on this?
(4) Are there any special problems for which he will need guidance?
(5) How broad a delegation can I make?

8. *PRINCIPLES OF EFFECTIVE COMMUNICATIONS*

(1) Determine the media
(2) To whom directed?
(3) Identification and source authority
(4) Is communication understood?

9. *PRINCIPLES OF WORK IMPROVEMENT*

(1) Most people usually do only the work which is assigned to them
(2) Workers are likely to fit assigned work into the time available to perform it
(3) A good workload usually stimulates output
(4) People usually do their best work when they know that results will be reviewed or inspected

(5) Employees usually feel that someone else is responsible for conditions of work, workplace layout, job methods, type of tools and equipment, and other such factors
(6) Employees are usually defensive about their job security
(7) Employees have natural resistance to change
(8) Employees can support or destroy a supervisor
(9) A supervisor usually earns the respect of his people through his personal example of diligence and efficiency

10. *AREAS OF JOB IMPROVEMENT*

The *areas* of job improvement are quite numerous, but the most common ones which a supervisor can identify and utilize are:

(1) Departmental layout
(2) Flow of work
(3) Workplace layout
(4) Utilization of manpower
(5) Work methods
(6) Materials handling
(7) Utilization
(8) Motion economy

11. *SEVEN KEY POINTS IN MAKING IMPROVEMENTS*

(1) Select the job to be improved
(2) Study how it is being done now
(3) Question the present method
(4) Determine actions to be taken
(5) Chart proposed method
(6) Get approval and apply
(7) Solicit worker participation

12. *CORRECTIVE TECHNIQUES OF JOB IMPROVEMENT*

Specific Problems	*General Problems*	*Corrective Technique*
(1) Size of workload	(1) Departmental layout	(1) Study with scale model
(2) Inability to meet schedules	(2) Flow of work	(2) Flow chart study
(3) Strain and fatigue	(3) Workplan layout	(3) Motion analysis
(4) Improper use of men and skills	(4) Utilization of manpower	(4) Comparison of units produced to standard allowances
(5) Waste, poor quality, unsafe conditions	(5) Work methods	(5) Methods analysis
(6) Bottleneck conditions that hinder output	(6) Materials handling	(6) Flow chart and equipment study
(7) Poor utilization of equipment and machines	(7) Utilization of equipment	(7) Down time vs. running time
(8) Efficiency and productivity of labor	(8) Motion economy	(8) Motion analysis

13. *A PLANNING CHECKLIST*

(1) Objectives
(2) Controls
(3) Delegations
(4) Communications
(5) Resources
(6) Methods and procedures
(7) Manpower
(8) Equipment
(9) Supplies and materials
(10) Utilization of time
(11) Safety
(12) Money
(13) Work
(14) Timing of improvements

14. *FIVE CHARACTERISTICS OF GOOD DIRECTIONS*

In order to get results, directions must be:

(1) Possible of accomplishment
(2) Agreeable with worker interests
(3) Related to mission
(4) Planned and complete
(5) Unmistakably clear

15. *TYPES OF DIRECTIONS*
        (1) Demands or direct orders (3) Suggestion or implication
        (2) Requests   (4) Volunteering

16. *CONTROLS*
    A typical listing of the overall areas in which the supervisor should establish controls might be:
        (1) Manpower   (4) Quantity of work (7) Money
        (2) Materials   (5) Time   (8) Methods
        (3) Quality of work (6) Space

17. *ORIENTING THE NEW EMPLOYEE*
        (1) Prepare for him   (3) Orientation for the job
        (2) Welcome the new employee (4) Follow-up

18. *CHECKLIST FOR ORIENTING NEW EMPLOYEES*

                                                      Yes No
        (1) Do your appreciate the feelings of new employees when they first report for work? ... ...
        (2) Are you aware of the fact that the new employee must make a big adjustment to his job? ... ...
        (3) Have you given him good reasons for liking the job and the organization? ... ...
        (4) Have you prepared for his first day on the job? ... ...
        (5) Did you welcome him cordially and make him feel needed? ... ...
        (6) Did you establish rapport with him so that he feels free to talk and discuss matters with you?... ...
        (7) Did you explain his job to him and his relationship to you? ... ...
        (8) Does he know that his work will be evaluated periodically on a basis that is fair and objective?.. ...
        (9) Did you introduce him to his fellow workers in such a way that they are likely to accept him? ... ...
     (10) Does he know what employee benefits he will receive? ... ...
     (11) Does he understand the importance of being on the job and what to do if he must leave his duty station? ... ...
     (12) Has he been impressed with the importance of accident prevention and safe practice? ... ...
     (13) Does he generally know his way around the department? ... ...
     (14) Is he under the guidance of a sponsor who will teach the right ways of doing things? ... ...
     (15) Do you plan to follow-up so that he will continue to adjust successfully to his job? ... ...

19. *PRINCIPLES OF LEARNING*
        (1) Motivation (2) Demonstration or explanation
        (3) Practice

20. *CAUSES OF POOR PERFORMANCE*
        (1) Improper training for job (6) Lack of standards of
        (2) Wrong tools   performance
        (3) Inadequate directions   (7) Wrong work habits
        (4) Lack of supervisory follow-up(8) Low morale
        (5) Poor communications   (9) Other

21. *FOUR MAJOR STEPS IN ON-THE-JOB INSTRUCTION*
        (1) Prepare the worker   (3) Tryout performance
        (2) Present the operation   (4) Follow-up

22. *EMPLOYEES WANT FIVE THINGS*
        (1) Security   (2) Opportunity   (3) Recognition
        (4) Inclusion   (5) Expression
23. *SOME DON'TS IN REGARD TO PRAISE*
        (1) Don't praise a person for something he hasn't done
        (2) Don't praise a person unless you can be sincere
        (3) Don't be sparing in praise just because your superior
            withholds it from you
        (4) Don't let too much time elapse between good performance
            and recognition of it
24. *HOW TO GAIN YOUR WORKERS' CONFIDENCE*
    Methods of developing confidence include such things as:
        (1) Knowing the interests, habits, hobbies of employees
        (2) Admitting your own inadequacies
        (3) Sharing and telling of confidence in others
        (4) Supporting people when they are in trouble
        (5) Delegating matters that can be well handled
        (6) Being frank and straightforward about problems and work-
            ing conditions
        (7) Encouraging others to bring their problems to you
        (8) Taking action on problems which impede worker progress
25. *SOURCES OF EMPLOYEE PROBLEMS*
    On-the-job causes might be such things as:
        (1) A feeling that favoritism is exercised in assignments
        (2) Assignment of overtime
        (3) An undue amount of supervision
        (4) Changing methods or systems
        (5) Stealing of ideas or trade secrets
        (6) Lack of interest in job
        (7) Threat of reduction in force
        (8) Ignorance or lack of communications
        (9) Poor equipment
      (10) Lack of knowing how supervisor feels toward employee
      (11) Shift assignments
    Off-the-job problems might have to do with:
        (1) Health (2) Finances (3) Housing (4) Family
26. *THE SUPERVISOR'S KEY TO DISCIPLINE*
    There are several key points about discipline which the super-
    visor should keep in mind:
        (1) Job discipline is one of the disciplines of life and is
            directed by the supervisor.
        (2) It is more important to correct an employee fault than to
            fix blame for it.
        (3) Employee performance is affected by problems both on the
            job and off.
        (4) Sudden or abrupt changes in behavior can be indications of
            important employee problems.
        (5) Problems should be dealt with as soon as possible after
            they are identified.
        (6) The attitude of the supervisor may have more to do with
            solving problems than the techniques of problem solving.
        (7) Correction of employee behavior should be resorted to only
            after the supervisor is sure that training or counseling
            will not be helpful
        (8) Be sure to document your disciplinary actions.

(9) Make sure that you are disciplining on the basis of facts rather than personal feelings.

(10) Take each disciplinary step in order, being careful not to make snap judgments, or decisions based on impatience.

27. *FIVE IMPORTANT PROCESSES OF MANAGEMENT*
    (1) Planning   (2) Organizing   (3) Scheduling
    (4) Controlling   (5) Motivating

28. *WHEN THE SUPERVISOR FAILS TO PLAN*
    (1) Supervisor creates impression of not knowing his job
    (2) May lead to excessive overtime
    (3) Job runs itself-- supervisor lacks control
    (4) Deadlines and appointments missed
    (5) Parts of the work go undone
    (6) Work interrupted by emergencies
    (7) Sets a bad example
    (8) Uneven workload creates peaks and valleys
    (9) Too much time on minor details at expense of more important tasks

29. *FOURTEEN GENERAL PRINCIPLES OF MANAGEMENT*

(1) Division of work	(8) Centralization
(2) Authority and responsibility	(9) Scalar chain
(3) Discipline	(10) Order
(4) Unity of command	(11) Equity
(5) Unity of direction	(12) Stability of tenure of personnel
(6) Subordination of individual interest to general interest	(13) Initiative
(7) Remuneration of personnel	(14) Esprit de corps

30. *CHANGE*

Bringing about change is perhaps attempted more often, and yet less well understood, than anything else the supervisor does. How do people generally react to change? (People tend to resist change that is imposed upon them by other individuals or circumstances.)

Change is characteristic of every situation. It is a part of **every** real endeavor where the efforts of people are concerned.

A. Why do people resist change?
    People may resist change because of:
      (1) Fear of the unknown
      (2) Implied criticism
      (3) Unpleasant experiences in the past
      (4) Fear of loss of status
      (5) Threat to the ego
      (6) Fear of loss of economic stability

B. How can we best overcome the resistance to change?
    In initiating change, take these steps:
      (1) Get ready to sell
      (2) identify sources of help
      (3) Anticipate objections
      (4) Sell benefits
      (5) Listen in depth
      (6) Follow up

B. BRIEF TOPICAL SUMMARIES

I. WHO/WHAT IS THE SUPERVISOR?

1. The supervisor is often called the "highest level employee and the lowest level manager."
2. A supervisor is a member of both management and the work group. He acts as a bridge between the two.
3. Most problems in supervision are in the area of human relations, or people problems.
4. Employees expect: Respect, opportunity to learn and to advance, and a sense of belonging, and so forth.
5. Supervisors are responsible for directing people and organizing work. Planning is of paramount importance.
6. A position description is a set of duties and responsibilities inherent to a given position.
7. It is important to keep the position description up-to-date and to provide each employee with his own copy.

II. THE SOCIOLOGY OF WORK

1. People are alike in many ways; however each individual is unique.
2. The supervisor is challenged in getting to know employee differences. Acquiring skills in evaluating individuals is an asset.
3. Maintaining meaningful working relationships in the organization is of great importance.
4. The supervisor has an obligation to help individuals to develop to their fullest potential.
5. Job rotation on a planned basis helps to build versatility and to maintain interest and enthusiasm in work groups.
6. Cross training (job rotation) provides backup skills.
7. The supervisor can help reduce tension by maintaining a sense of humor, providing guidance to employees, and by making reasonable and timely decisions. Employees respond favorably to working under reasonably predictable circumstances.
8. Change is characteristic of all managerial behavior. The supervisor must adjust to changes in procedures, new methods, technological changes, and to a number of new and sometimes challenging situations.
9. To overcome the natural tendency for people to resist change, the supervisor should become more skillful in initiating change.

III. PRINCIPLES AND PRACTICES OF SUPERVISION

1. Employees should be required to answer to only one superior.
2. A supervisor can effectively direct only a limited number of employees, depending upon the complexity, variety, and proximity of the jobs involved.
3. The organizational chart presents the organization in graphic form. It reflects lines of authority and responsibility as well as interrelationships of units within the organization.
4. Distribution of work can be improved through an analysis using the "Work Distribution Chart."
5. The "Work Distribution Chart" reflects the division of work within a unit in understandable form.
6. When related tasks are given to an employee, he has a better chance of increasing his skills through training.
7. The individual who is given the responsibility for tasks must also be given the appropriate authority to insure adequate results.
8. The supervisor should delegate repetitive, routine work. Preparation of recurring reports, maintaining leave and attendance records are some examples.

11

9. Good discipline is essential to good task performance. Discipline is reflected in the actions of employees on the job in the absence of supervision.
10. Disciplinary action may have to be taken when the positive aspects of discipline have failed. Reprimand, warning, and suspension are examples of disciplinary action.
11. If a situation calls for a reprimand, be sure it is deserved and remember it is to be done in private.

IV. DYNAMIC LEADERSHIP
1. A style is a personal method or manner of exerting influence.
2. Authoritarian leaders often see themselves as the source of power and authority.
3. The democratic leader often perceives the group as the source of authority and power.
4. Supervisors tend to do better when using the pattern of leadership that is most natural for them.
5. Social scientists suggest that the effective supervisor use the leadership style that best fits the problem or circumstances involved.
6. All four styles -- telling, selling, consulting, joining -- have their place. Using one does not preclude using the other at another time.
7. The theory X point of view assumes that the average person dislikes work, will avoid it whenever possible, and must be coerced to achieve organizational objectives.
8. The theory Y point of view assumes that the average person considers work to be as natural as play, and, when the individual is committed, he requires little supervision or direction to accomplish desired objectives.
9. The leader's basic assumptions concerning human behavior and human nature affect his actions, decisions, and other managerial practices.
10. Dissatisfaction among employees is often present, but difficult to isolate. The supervisor should seek to weaken dissatisfaction by keeping promises, being sincere and considerate, keeping employees informed, and so forth.
11. Constructive suggestions should be encouraged during the natural progress of the work.

V. PROCESSES FOR SOLVING PROBLEMS
1. People find their daily tasks more meaningful and satisfying when they can improve them.
2. The causes of problems, or the key factors, are often hidden in the background. Ability to solve problems often involves the ability to isolate them from their backgrounds. There is some substance to the cliché that some persons "can't see the forest for the trees."
3. New procedures are often developed from old ones. Problems should be broken down into manageable parts. New ideas can be adapted from old ones.
4. People think differently in problem-solving situations. Using a logical, patterned approach is often useful. One approach found to be useful includes these steps:
   (a) Define the problem   (d) Weigh and decide
   (b) Establish objectives   (e) Take action
   (c) Get the facts   (f) Evaluate action

12

VI. TRAINING FOR RESULTS

1. Participants respond best when they feel training is important to them.
2. The supervisor has responsibility for the training and development of those who report to him.
3. When training is delegated to others, great care must be exercised to insure the trainer has knowledge, aptitude, and interest for his work as a trainer.
4. Training (learning) of some type goes on continually. The most successful supervisor makes certain the learning contributes in a productive manner to operational goals.
5. New employees are particularly susceptible to training. Older employees facing new job situations require specific training, as well as having need for development and growth opportunities.
6. Training needs require continuous monitoring.
7. The training officer of an agency is a professional with a responsibility to assist supervisors in solving training problems.
8. Many of the self-development steps important to the supervisor's own growth are equally important to the development of peers and subordinates. Knowledge of these is important when the supervisor consults with others on development and growth opportunities.

VII. HEALTH, SAFETY, AND ACCIDENT PREVENTION

1. Management-minded supervisors take appropriate measures to assist employees in maintaining health and in assuring safe practices in the work environment.
2. Effective safety training and practices help to avoid injury and accidents.
3. Safety should be a management goal. All infractions of safety which are observed should be corrected without exception.
4. Employees' safety attitude, training and instruction, provision of safe tools and equipment, supervision, and leadership are considered highly important factors which contribute to safety and which can be influenced directly by supervisors.
5. When accidents do occur they should be investigated promptly for very important reasons, including the fact that information which is gained can be used to prevent accidents in the future.

VIII. EQUAL EMPLOYMENT OPPORTUNITY

1. The supervisor should endeavor to treat all employees fairly, without regard to religion, race, sex, or national origin.
2. Groups tend to reflect the attitude of the leader. Prejudice can be detected even in very subtle form. Supervisors must strive to create a feeling of mutual respect and confidence in every employee.
3. Complete utilization of all human resources is a national goal. Equitable consideration should be accorded women in the work force, minority-group members, the physically and mentally handicapped, and the older employee. The important question is: "Who can do the job?"
4. Training opportunities, recognition for performance, overtime assignments, promotional opportunities, and all other personnel actions are to be handled on an equitable basis.

IX. IMPROVING COMMUNICATIONS
1. Communications is achieving understanding between the sender and the receiver of a message. It also means sharing information -- the creation of understanding.
2. Communication is basic to all human activity. Words are means of conveying meanings; however, real meanings are in people.
3. There are very practical differences in the effectiveness of one-way, impersonal, and two-way communications. Words spoken face-to-face are better understood. Telephone conversations are effective, but lack the rapport of person-to-person exchanges. The whole person communicates.
4. Cooperation and communication in an organization go hand-in-hand. When there is a mutual respect between people, spelling out rules and procedures for communicating is unnecessary.
5. There are several barriers to effective communications. These include failure to listen with respect and understanding, lack of skill in feedback, and misinterpreting the meanings of words used by the speaker. It is also common practice to listen to what we want to hear, and tune out things we do not want to hear.
6. Communication is management's chief problem. The supervisor should accept the challenge to communicate more effectively and to improve interagency and intra-agency communications.
7. The supervisor may often plan for and conduct meetings. The planning phase is critical and may determine the success or the failure of a meeting.
8. Speaking before groups usually requires extra effort. Stage fright may never disappear completely, but it can be controlled.

X. SELF-DEVELOPMENT
1. Every employee is responsible for his own self-development.
2. Toastmaster and toastmistress clubs offer opportunities to improve skills in oral communications.
3. Planning for one's own self-development is of vital importance. Supervisors know their own strengths and limitations better than anyone else.
4. Many opportunities are open to aid the supervisor in his developmental efforts, including job assignments; training opportunities, both governmental and non-governmental -- to include universities and professional conferences and seminars.
5. Programmed instruction offers a means of studying at one's own rate.
6. Where difficulties may arise from a supervisor's being away from his work for training, he may participate in televised home study or correspondence courses to meet his self-development needs.

XI. TEACHING AND TRAINING
A. The Teaching Process
Teaching is encouraging and guiding the learning activities of students toward established goals. In most cases this process consists in five steps: preparation, presentation, summarization, evaluation, and application.

1. Preparation

Preparation is twofold in nature; that of the supervisor and the employee.

Preparation by the supervisor is absolutely essential to success. He must know what, when, where, how, and whom he will teach. Some of the factors that should be considered are:

(1) The objectives   (5) Employee interest
(2) The materials needed   (6) Training aids
(3) The methods to be used   (7) Evaluation
(4) Employee participation   (8) Summarization

Employee preparation consists in preparing the employee to receive the material. Probably the most important single factor in the preparation of the employee is arousing and maintaining his interest. He must know the objectives of the training, why he is there, how the material can be used, and its importance to him.

2. Presentation

In presentation, have a carefully designed plan and follow it. The plan should be accurate and complete, yet flexible enough to meet situations as they arise. The method of presentation will be determined by the particular situation and objectives.

3. Summary

A summary should be made at the end of every training unit and program. In addition, there may be internal summaries depending on the nature of the material being taught. The important thing is that the trainee must always be able to understand how each part of the new material relates to the whole.

4. Application

The supervisor must arrange work so the employee will be given a chance to apply new knowledge or skills while the material is still clear in his mind and interest is high. The trainee does not really know whether he has learned the material until he has been given a chance to apply it. If the material is not applied, it loses most of its value.

5. Evaluation

The purpose of all training is to promote learning. To determine whether the training has been a success or failure, the supervisor must evaluate this learning.

In the broadest sense evaluation includes all the devices, methods, skills, and techniques used by the supervisor to keep himself and the employees informed as to their progress toward the objectives they are pursuing. The extent to which the employee has mastered the knowledge, skills, and abilities, or changed his attitudes, as determined by the program objectives, is the extent to which instruction has succeeded or failed.

Evaluation should not be confined to the end of the lesson, day, or program but should be used continuously. We shall note later the way this relates to the rest of the teaching process.

B. Teaching Methods

A teaching method is a pattern of identifiable student and instructor activity used in presenting training material.

All supervisors are faced with the problem of deciding which method should be used at a given time.

1. Lecture
   The lecture is direct oral presentation of material by the supervisor. The present trend is to place less emphasis on the trainer's activity and more on that of the trainee.
2. Discussion
   Teaching by discussion or conference involves using questions and other techniques to arouse interest and focus attention upon certain areas, and by doing so creating a learning situation. This can be one of the most valuable methods because it gives the employees an opportunity to express their ideas and pool their knowledge.
3. Demonstration
   The demonstration is used to teach how something works or how to do something. It can be used to show a principle or what the results of a series of actions will be. A well-staged demonstration is particularly effective because it shows proper methods of performance in a realistic manner.
4. Performance
   Performance is one of the most fundamental of all learning techniques or teaching methods. The trainee may be able to tell how a specific operation should be performed but he cannot be sure he knows how to perform the operation until he has done so.

As with all methods, there are certain advantages and disadvantages to each method.

5. Which Method to Use
   Moreover, there are other methods and techniques of teaching. It is difficult to use any method without other methods entering into it. In any learning situation a combination of methods is usually more effective than any one method alone.

Finally, evaluation must be integrated into the other aspects of the teaching-learning process.

It must be used in the motivation of the trainees; it must be used to assist in developing understanding during the training; and it must be related to employee application of the results of training.

This is distinctly the role of the supervisor.

———

BASIC FUNDAMENTALS OF LIBRARY SCIENCE

The problem of classifying all human knowledge has produced a branch of learning called "library science." A lasting contribution to a simple and understandable method of locating a book on any topic was designed by Melvil Dewey in 1876. His plan divided all knowledge into ten large classes and then dubdivided each class according to related groups.

DEWEY DECIMAL SYSTEM

1. Subject Classification

   The Dewey Decimal Classification System is the accepted and most widely used subject classification system in libraries throughout the world.

2. Classification by Three (3) Groups

   There are three groups of classification in the system. A basic group of ten (10) classifications arranges all knowledge as represented by books within groups by classifications numbered 000-900.

   The second group is the "100 division"; each group of the basic "10 divisions" is again divided into 9 sub-sctions allowing for more detailed and specialized subjects not identified in the 10 basic divisions.

3. There is a third, still further specialized "One thousand" group where each of the "100" classifications are further divided by decimalized, more specified, subject classifications. The "1,000" group is mainly used by highly specialized scientific and much diversified libraries.

   These are the subject classes of the Dewey System:

000-099	General works (included bibliography, encyclopedias, collections, periodicals, newspapers,etc.)
100-199	Philosophy (includes psychology,logic,ethics,conduct,etc.)
200-299	Religion (includes mythology,natural theology,Bible,church history,etc.)
300-399	Social Science (includes economics,government,law,education,commerce,etc.)
400-499	Language (includes dictionaries,grammars,philology,etc.)
500-599	Science (includes mathematics,chemistry,physics,astronomy, geology,etc.)
600-699	Useful Arts (includes agriculture,engineering,aviation, medicine,manufactures,etc.)
700-799	Fine Arts (includes sculpture,painting,music,photography, gardening,etc.)
800-899	Literature (includes poetry,plays,orations,etc.)
900-999	History (includes geoegraphy,travel,biography,ancient and modern history,etc.)

PREPARING TO USE THE LIBRARY

Your ability to use the library and its resources is an important factor in determining your success. Skill and efficiency in finding the library materials you need for assignments and research papers will increase the amount of time you have to devote to reading or organizing information.
These are some of the preparations you can make now.

1. Develop skill in using your local library. You can increase your familiarity with the card catalog and the periodical indexes, such as the *Readers' Guide to Periodical Literature,* in any library.
2. Take the *Test in Library Science* to see how you can improve your knowledge of the library.

3. Read in such books as *Books, Libraries and You* by Jessie Edna Boyd, *The Library Key* by Margaret G. Cook, and *Making Books Work, a Guide to the Use of Libraries* by Jennie Maas Flexner.

You can find other titles by looking under the subject heading LIBRARIES AND READERS in the card catalog of your library.

THREE TYPES OF BOOK CARDS

Here are the three general types of cards which are used to represent a book in the main catalog.

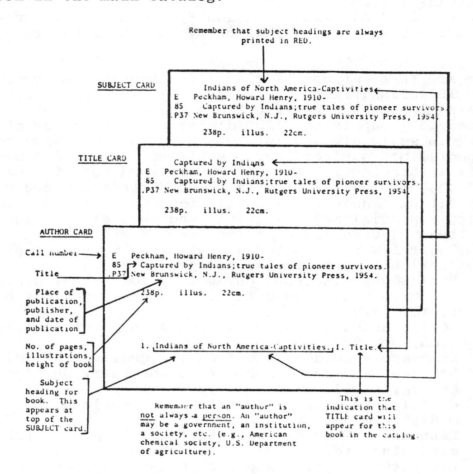

CARD CATALOG

The Card Catalog lists all books in the library by author. The majority of books also have title and subject cards.

<u>Author card</u>

If the author is known, look in the catalog under the author's name. The "author" for some works may be a society, an institution, or a government department.

<u>Title card</u>

Books with distinctive titles, anonymous works and periodicals will have a title card.

<u>Subject card</u>

To find books on a specific subject, look in the catalog under that subject heading. (Subject headings are printed in red on the Catalog Card.)

<u>Call number</u>
The letters and numbers in the upper left-hand corner of the Catalog Card are the book's call number. Copy this call number accurately,
for it will determine the shelf location of the book. The word "Reference" marked in red in the upper right-hand corner of the catalog card
indicates that the item is shelved in the Reference Section, and "Periodical "marked in yellow on the Catalog Card indicates that the item is
shelved in the Periodicals Section.
PERIODICALS
All magazines are arranged in alphabetical order by title.
PERIODICALS FILE
To determine whether the Library has a specific magazine, consult the
Periodicals File. Check the title of the magazine needed, and note that
there are two cards for each title.
The bottom card lists the current issues available. The top card
lists back bound volumes.
Those marked "Ask at Ref.Desk" may be obtained from the Reference
Librarian.
PERIODICAL INDEXES
Material in magazines is more up-to-date than books and is a valuable
source of information. To find articles on a chosen subject, use the pe-
riodical indexes.
The Readers'Guide to Periodical Literature is the most familiar of
these indexes. In the front of each volume is a list of the periodicals
indexed and a key to abbreviations. Similar aids appear in the front of
other periodical indexes.
Sample entry: WEASELS
              WONDERFUL WHITE WEASEL. R.Beck. il OUTDOOR LIFE
              135:48-9+ Ja '65
Explanation : An illustrated article on the subject WEASELS entitled
              WONDERFUL WHITE WEASEL, by R.Beck, will be found in
              volume 135 of OUTDOOR LIFE, pages 48-9 (continued on la-
              ter pages of the same issue), the January 1965 number.
Major libraries subscribe to the following indexes:
<u>Art Index</u>
<u>Biography Index</u>
<u>Book Review Index</u>
<u>British Humanities Index</u>
<u>Essay and General Literature Index</u>
This is helpful for locating criticism of works of literature.
<u>An Index to Book Reviews in the Humanities</u>
<u>International Index</u> ceased publications June, 1965 and continued
as <u>Social Science and Humanities Index</u>
<u>The Music Index</u>
<u>The New York Times Index</u>
<u>Nineteenth Century Readers' Guide</u>
<u>Poole's Index</u>
<u>Poverty and Human Resources Abstracts</u>
<u>Psychological Abstracts</u>
<u>Public Affairs Information Service, Bulletin of the (PAIS)</u> is a sub-
ject index to current books, pamphlets, periodical articles, government documents, and other library materials in economics and public
affairs.
<u>Readers' Guide to Periodical Literature</u>
<u>Social Science and Humanities Index</u> a continuation of the <u>Interna-
tional Index</u>
<u>Sociological Abstracts</u>

Do you have the basic skills for using a library efficiently? You should be able to answer AT LEAST 33 of the following questions correctly. *CHECK YOUR ANSWERS BY TURNING TO THE ANSWER KEY AT THE BACK OF THIS SECTION.*

I. USING A CARD CATALOG

Questions 1-9.

DIRECTIONS: An author card (or "main entry" card) is shown below. Identify each item on the card by selecting the CORRECT letters for them. *PRINT THE LETTER OF THE CORRECT ANSWER IN THE SPACE AT THE RIGHT.*

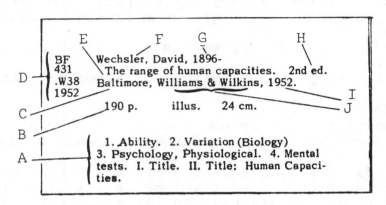

Sample Answer:
0.   F

1. Date book was published.   1. ...
2. Number of pages in book.   2. ...
3. Title.   3. ...
4. Place of publication.   4. ...
5. Call number.   5. ...
6. Year author was born,   6. ...
7. Edition.   7. ...
8. Publisher.   8. ...
9. Other headings under which cards for this book may be   9. ...
   found.

Questions 10-13.

DIRECTIONS: Select the letter preceding the word or phrase which completes each of the following statements correctly.

10. The library's title card for the book THE LATE GEORGE AP-   10. ...
    LEY can be found by looking in the card catalog under
        A. Apley,George   B. The   C. Late   D. George   E. Apley

11. A catalog card for a book by John F. Kennedy would be   11. ...
    found in the drawer labelled
        A. JEFFERSON-JOHNSON,ROY
        B. PRESCOTT-PRICELESS
        C. KIERNAN-KLAY
        D. U.S.PRESIDENT-U.S.SOCIAL SECURITY
        E. KENNEBEC-KIERKEGAARD

4

12. The title cards for these three periodicals would be found 12. ...
    in the card catalog arranged in which of the following orders:
        A. NEW YORKER, NEWSWEEK, NEW YORK TIMES MAGAZINE
        B. NEWSWEEK, NEW YORKER, NEW YORK TIMES MAGAZINE
        C. NEW YORK TIMES MAGAZINE, NEW YORKER, NEWSWEEK
        D. NEW YORKER, NEW YORK TIMES MAGAZINE, NEWSWEEK
        E. NEWSWEEK, NEW YORK TIMES MAGAZINE, NEW YORKER
13. A card for a copy of the U.N. Charter would be found in the 13. ...
    catalog drawer marked
        A. TWENTIETH-UNAMUNO
        B. UNITED MINE WORKERS-UNITED SHOE MACHINERY
        C. U.S. BUREAU-U.S. CONGRESS
        D. U.S. SOCIAL POLICY-UNIVERSITAS
        E. CHANCEL-CIARDI

II. UNDERSTANDING ENTRIES IN A PERIODICAL INDEX
    Questions 14-25.
    DIRECTIONS: The following items are excerpts from THE READERS'
               GUIDE TO PERIODICAL LITERATURE. Identify each lettered
               section of the entries by placing the correct letters
               in the spaces. (There are more letters than spaces, so
               some of the letters will not be used.)

A____UNITED NATIONS
     Ambassador Goldberg holds news conference at
       New York; transcript of conference,
B____July 28, 1965; with questions and answers.
       A. J. Goldberg. Dept. State Bul 53:272+
C____ Ag 16 '65
     U.N. out of its teens. I.D. Talmadge. il Sr Schol
E____ 87:16-17+ S 16 '65
D____ Whatever became of the United Nations?
       America 113:235 S 4 '65

        F   R
                Charter
     Up-dating the pre-atomic United Nations; address,
       June 20, 1965. C.P. Romulo. Vital Speeches
       31:658-61 Ag 15 '65; Excerpts. Sat R 48:34-5+
       Jl 24 '65
                        N
                 G

H_____Security Council
     Security Council urged to respond to
       challenge in southeast Asia; letter,
M____July 30, 1965. A. J. Goldberg. Dept
     State Bul 53:278-80+ Ag 16, '65

        L   •I   J K

14. Title of magazine containing a transcript of a news con-   14. ...
    conference held by U.N. Ambassador Arthur Goldberg.
15. Magazine in which the full text of C.P. Romulo's address   15.
    on the U.N. appears.
16. Author of an article titled U.N. OUT OF ITS TEENS.   16. ...
17. Date on which Ambassador Goldberg wrote a letter urging   17. ...
    the Security Council to respond to the challenge of south-
    east Asia.
18. Title of an article for which no author is listed.   18. ...
19. Date of the SATURDAY REVIEW issue which contains excerpts   19. ...
    of a speech called "Up-Dating the Pre-Atomic United Nations."
20. Pages in the DEPARTMENT OF STATE BULLETIN on which Am-   20. ...
    bassador Goldberg's letter appears.
21. Symbol indicating that the letter is continued on a la-   21. ...
    ter page.
22. Volume number of the magazine in which the article by   22. ...
    I.D. Talmadge is printed.
23. Symbols meaning September 16, 1965.   23. ...

24. The general subject heading under which all five articles   24. ...
    are listed.
25. A subject heading subdivision.   25. ...
Questions 26-27.
DIRECTIONS: Select the letter preceding the phrase which completes
            each of the following statements correctly.
26. To determine whether or not the library has THE MAGAZINE OF 26. ...
    AMERICAN HISTORY, check in
        A. the list of magazine titles in the front of THE REA-
           DERS' GUIDE TO PERIODICAL LITERATURE
        B. the library's card catalog
        C. Ulrich's GUIDE TO PERIODICALS
        D. SATURDAY REVIEW
        E. THE LIBRARY JOURNAL
27. THE READERS' GUIDE is a good place to look for material on   27. ...
    the Job Corps because it
        A. indexes only the best books and magazines in each field
        B. is a guide to articles on many subjects appearing in
           all of the library's periodicals
        C. indexes recent discussions on the subject in many maga-
           zines
        D. specializes in official government information
        E. does all of the above
III. IDENTIFYING LIBRARY TERMS
     Questions 28-32.
     DIRECTIONS: Match the correct definitions with these terms
                 by placing the correct letters in the blanks.
                 (Some of the letters will not be used.)

28. Bibliography   A. Word or phrase printed in   28. ...
29. Anthology   red at the top of a cata-   29. ...
30. Index   log to indicate the major   30. ...
31. Abstract   topic of the book   31. ...
32. Subject heading   B. Brief written summary of   32. ...
                             the major ideas presented
                             in an article or book
                          C. List of books and/or arti-
                             cles on one subject or
                             by one author
                          D. Collection of selections from
                             the writings of one or sever-
                             al authors
                          E. Written account of a person's
                             life
                          F. Alphabetical list of subjects
                             with the pages on which they
                             are to be found in a book or
                             periodical
                          G. Subordinate,usually explanatory
                             title,additional to the main
                             title and usually printed be-
                             low it

IV. FINDING A BOOK BY ITS CALL NUMBER

Questions 33-38.

DIRECTIONS: The Library of Congress classification system call numbers shown below are arranged in order, just as the books bearing those call numbers would be arranged on the shelves. To show where other call numbers would be located, select the letter of the CORRECT ANSWER.

A.	B.	C.	D.	E.	F.	G.	H.	I.	J.	K.
PS	PS	PS	PS	PS	PS	PS	PS	PS	PS	PS
201	201	208	351	351	3513	3515	3515.3	3526	3526.17	3526.37
.L67	.M44	.B87	.D7	.D77	.A2	.D72	A66	.N21	P2	A10
1961		1944								

L.	M.	N.
PS	PS	PT
3526.37	3526.37	1
C20	C37	.R2

33. A book with the call number PS 201 .L67 would be shelved   33. ...

    A. Before A   B. Between A & B   C. Between B & C
    D. Between C & D   E. Between D & E

34, A book with the call number PS 208 .B87 1944a would be shelved   34. ...

    A. Between A & B B. Between C & D   C. Between B & C
    D. Between C & D E. Between D & E

35. A book with the call number PS 351 .D8 would be shelved   35. ...

    A. Between C & D B. Between D & E   C. Between E & F
    D. Between F & G E. Between G & H

36. A book with the call number PS 3526.3 M53 would be shelved   36. ...

    A. Between L & M B. Between J & K   C. Between K & L
    D. Between M & O E. Between O & P

37. A book with the call number PS 3526.37 C205 would be shelved   37. ...

    A. Between L & M B. Between N & O   C. Between M & N
    D. Between O & P E. Between P & Q

38. A book with the call number PS 3526.37 C3 would be shelved   38. ...

    A. Between M & N B. Between L & M   C. Between N & O
    D. Between O & P D. Between P & Q

V. General
    Questions 39-40.
    DIRECTIONS: Each question or incomplete statement is followed by
               several suggested answers or completions. Select the
               one that BEST answers the question or completes the
               statement. *PRINT THE LETTER OF THE CORRECT ANSWER IN
               THE SPACE AT THE RIGHT.*
39. When it is finished (in 610 volumes), the _____   39. ...
    will be the MOST monumental national bibliography in the
    world.
        A. UNION LIST OF SERIALS IN LIBRARIES OF THE UNITED
            STATES AND CANADA
        B. UNITED STATES CATALOG
        C. READERS' GUIDE TO PERIODICAL LITERATURE
        D. NATIONAL UNION CATALOG
40. For those who wish to investigate the publishing com-   40. ...
    panies and the people who control them, to locate the
    date a company was founded, who owned it, when it changed
    hands, what firm succeeded it, and other information of a
    similar nature, the periodical _____ is clearly
    invaluable.
        A. PUBLISHERS' TRADE LIST ANNUAL (PTLA)
        B. CUMULATIVE BOOK INDEX
        C. AMERICAN BOOKTRADE DIRECTORY
        D. PUBLISHERS WEEKLY

KEY (CORRECT ANSWERS)

1. I   2. B   3. E   4. C   5. D   6. G   7. H   8. J   9. A
10. C - The first word of the title which is not an article.
11. E - Every book in the library is listed in the card catalog under
        the author's name. (Warning: The "author" may be a society, a
        university, or some other institution.)
12. C - A title is alphabetized word-by-word; therefore,"New" comes
        before "Newsweek," "New York" before "New Yorker."
13. B - The United Nations,not an individual,is the author of this work.
14. T   16. Q   18. D   20. J   22. E   24. A   26. B   28. C   30. F   32. A
15. O   17. M   19. N   21. K   23. R   25. P/H   27. C   29. D   31. B
33. A - When two call numbers are identical except that one has a year
        or some other figure added at its end, the shorter call numbers
        comes first.
34. B
35. C - The numbers which follow a. are regarded as decimals; therefore,
        .D77 precedes .D8.
36. B - 3526.3 precedes 3526.37
37. A - .C20 precedes .C205
38. B - .C3 precedes .C37
    (Read the call number line-by-line, and put a J before a P, before a
     PB, etc. Put a lower number before a greater one.)
39. D
40. D

ANSWER SHEET

TEST NO. ________________ PART ______ TITLE OF POSITION ________________________________
(AS GIVEN IN EXAMINATION ANNOUNCEMENT - INCLUDE OPTION, IF ANY)

PLACE OF EXAMINATION ________________________________ ________________ DATE ________
(CITY OR TOWN) (STATE)

RATING

USE THE SPECIAL PENCIL. MAKE GLOSSY BLACK MARKS.

1 A B C D E	26 A B C D E	51 A B C D E	76 A B C D E	101 A B C D E
2 A B C D E	27 A B C D E	52 A B C D E	77 A B C D E	102 A B C D E
3 A B C D E	28 A B C D E	53 A B C D E	78 A B C D E	103 A B C D E
4 A B C D E	29 A B C D E	54 A B C D E	79 A B C D E	104 A B C D E
5 A B C D E	30 A B C D E	55 A B C D E	80 A B C D E	105 A B C D E
6 A B C D E	31 A B C D E	56 A B C D E	81 A B C D E	106 A B C D E
7 A B C D E	32 A B C D E	57 A B C D E	82 A B C D E	107 A B C D E
8 A B C D E	33 A B C D E	58 A B C D E	83 A B C D E	108 A B C D E
9 A B C D E	34 A B C D E	59 A B C D E	84 A B C D E	109 A B C D E
10 A B C D E	35 A B C D E	60 A B C D E	85 A B C D E	110 A B C D E

Make only ONE mark for each answer. Additional and stray marks may be counted as mistakes. In making corrections, erase errors COMPLETELY.

11 A B C D E	36 A B C D E	61 A B C D E	86 A B C D E	111 A B C D E
12 A B C D E	37 A B C D E	62 A B C D E	87 A B C D E	112 A B C D E
13 A B C D E	38 A B C D E	63 A B C D E	88 A B C D E	113 A B C D E
14 A B C D E	39 A B C D E	64 A B C D E	89 A B C D E	114 A B C D E
15 A B C D E	40 A B C D E	65 A B C D E	90 A B C D E	115 A B C D E
16 A B C D E	41 A B C D E	66 A B C D E	91 A B C D E	116 A B C D E
17 A B C D E	42 A B C D E	67 A B C D E	92 A B C D E	117 A B C D E
18 A B C D E	43 A B C D E	68 A B C D E	93 A B C D E	118 A B C D E
19 A B C D E	44 A B C D E	69 A B C D E	94 A B C D E	119 A B C D E
20 A B C D E	45 A B C D E	70 A B C D E	95 A B C D E	120 A B C D E
21 A B C D E	46 A B C D E	71 A B C D E	96 A B C D E	121 A B C D E
22 A B C D E	47 A B C D E	72 A B C D E	97 A B C D E	122 A B C D E
23 A B C D E	48 A B C D E	73 A B C D E	98 A B C D E	123 A B C D E
24 A B C D E	49 A B C D E	74 A B C D E	99 A B C D E	124 A B C D E
25 A B C D E	50 A B C D E	75 A B C D E	100 A B C D E	125 A B C D E

ANSWER SHEET

TEST NO. _____ PART _____ TITLE OF POSITION _____

PLACE OF EXAMINATION _____ DATE _____

(CITY OR TOWN)   (STATE)

RATING

USE THE SPECIAL PENCIL.   MAKE GLOSSY BLACK MARKS.

Make only ONE mark for each answer.   Additional and stray marks may be counted as mistakes.   In making corrections, erase errors COMPLETELY.